THE CASUAL
PRESENCE
OF BORDERS

University of New Orleans Press
Manufactured in the United States of America
ISBN: 978-1-60801-178-0

Book and cover design by Alex Dimeff

Some of the following poems appear under different titles herein, and some may have been slightly revised herein:

Mackie Blanton. Four Poems: "Make Tomorrow Come," "The Presence of An Idea," "Eve on the Riverfront," "Cornered." The Southern Conference on Linguistics. *The Southern Journal of Linguistics*, 36.1: 186-190. Christina Schoux Casey, Editor. 2012.

Mackie Blanton. "Bloody Borders". *Chicken Bones: A Journal for Literary and Artistic African-American Themes*. The Nathaniel Turner Online Index. Rudolph Lewis, Editor. 2008.

Mackie Blanton. 2008. "The Struggle Ode". *Chicken Bones: A Journal for Literary and Artistic African-American Themes*. The Nathaniel Turner Online Index. Rudolph Lewis, Editor. 2008.

Mackie Blanton. 2006. "Neighbors and Invaders". *Chicken Bones: An Online Journal for Literary and Artistic African-American Themes*. The Nathaniel Turner Online Index. Rudolph Lewis, Editor. 2006.

Mackie Blanton. "Malcolm's Landing: A Labor Day Lament". *Chicken Bones: A Journal for Literary and Artistic African-American Themes*. The Nathaniel Turner Online Index. Rudolph Lewis, Editor. 2006.

Mackie Blanton. "Five Haikus," & Photography. *The Southern University of New Orleans Revue*. Vol. 2. 2001.

Mackie Blanton. "Tearoses and Pursestrings". *Cricket: Poems and Other Jazz*, Vol. 1, No. 1. Elaine Leyda, Editor. University of Louisiana at Lafayette. 1986.

Mackie Blanton. "The Coop of God." *The Southwestern Review*, Vol. 8, No. 11. 1983.

Mackie Blanton. First and Second Place Poetry Award. Humanities Department Lewis Poetry Prizes. Illinois Institute of Technology, Chicago, IL 60616. 1970.

Mackie Blanton. Second Place Poetry Award. Humanities Department Lewis Poetry Prizes. Illinois Institute of Technology, Chicago, IL 60616. 1968.

THE UNIVERSITY OF NEW ORLEANS PRESS
unopress.org

THE CASUAL
PRESENCE
OF BORDERS

poems

Mackie J.V. Blanton

To Linda and Jordan, each both my border and my frontier

ACKNOWLEDGMENTS

I am extremely grateful to the leadership and the capable hands at the UNO Press: Abram Shalom Himelstein, Editor-in-Chief; George K. Darby, Managing Editor; Book and Cover Designer and Typesetter *par excellence*, Alex Dimeff.

I wish to inscribe here in chronological order the names of individuals who in a conversation's single split-second once uttered an insight emerging almost out of my awareness in passing about life, teaching, art, and literature. Each such single incident has stuck with me deeply over many decades or recent years. I also would like to think Sondra Sue Cloth Reine, Lila June Courtney Riley, and Gerie Nelson Levy, Honorary Members of The New Orleans Black Golden Girls Detective Agency, for jogging my memory about the first names of certain Xavier University Professors inscribed at or near the top of my list (2nd through 8th).

Fr. Gordon Hughes, S.S.J., Léon Baisier, Hamilton P. Avengo, Robert K. Kramer, Helen C. Caniff, Leo de Alvarez, Numa Rousseve, Oscar Bouise, Henry De Laune, Paul Brosman, John T. Scott, Gene Kidd, George Entenman, Art Spring, Laurence Michalak, James Cooney, Robert Ruggill, Pierre Chanover, Al Davis, Bill Austin, Vernon Losee, John Root, Roger Gilman, Dennis Peacock, Mary Moulton, Linda H. Hillman, Laura Hellwig, Doug Kent Stuart, Rubiyah Spinka, David Queen, Frank Giacobbi, Vahe Baladouni, John R.O. Gery, Rudy Lewis, Deborah Cains, William Middleton, Staffas Broussard, Greta Gladney, Ralph Chandler, Jeremy Kerr, David Gregorio Fleitas-Velez, John Vassilopoulos, Bill Manaris, Niyi Osundare, John Randolph, Marie Randolph, Joyce Soyohatta King Maiga, Hassimi Oumarou Maiga, Anne Teachworth, Jeff Teachworth, Kenneth Supman, Lenny Ravich, Morgan Goodlander, George Dorrill, Bob Maurice, James Cagle, Members of the Northshore Cosmology & Consciousness Studies Group, Roslyn R. Foy, Edmond J. Foy, Kevin McNamara, Christina Schoux Casey, Patrick Thomas Casey, David Hanson, Rebecca Hite, Richard Louth, Dayne Sherman, Eulalia Eco Vittitow.

Those who see the truth and call it a lie are fools. Those who tell or see a lie and call it the truth are criminals (Bertolt Brecht. *Life of Galileo*. 1938 [First Theatrical Production in German 9 September 1943]).

A mind that is indifferent is aware of the shoddiness of our civilization, of the street, of a smile; but merely observes with that warm affectionate indifference. Observation is not detachment, because there is no attachment. It is only when the mind is attached that you talk about detachment. But, you know, when you are indifferent, there is a sweetness to it, there is a perfume to it, there is a quality of tremendous energy. One has to be indifferent. Indifference comes into being when you listen to that noise with no resistance, go with that noise, ride on that noise infinitely. You listen to every noise in the world completely with indifference and therefore with Understanding (J. Krishnamurti. Observation is Not Detachment. 6th Public Talk, Bombay, 7 March 1962).

Those who seek the Spirit's light should never form themselves into a 'congregation', because no congregation can exist without enforcement of beliefs; and there is nothing less conducive to the soul's unfolding than all external pressure to "believe" .... Congregations of whatever kind are nothing more than funeral processions of their members' perished faith (BÔ YIN RÂ. "The Secret Temple." *The Book on the Living God*, 2/ed. 1992, 149–150).

When I wished to find knowledge of the secrets of Creation, I came upon a dark vault within the depths of the earth, filled with blowing winds .... Then there appeared to me in my sleep a shape of most wondrous beauty [giving me instructions on how to conduct myself in order to attain knowledge of the highest things]. I then said to him: "Who are you?" And he answered: "I am your perfected nature" (*Hermes*. Gershom Scholem. 1991, 55).

BORDERS AND GATES

III. SWERVE SWAY SWOON

IV. AT A LOSS FOR WORDS

V. MONUMENTS AND RUINS

VI. A GATEFOLD CELEBRATION

VII. TIDES OF MIND

VIII. IMMORTAL ARCHEAOLOGY

IX. LISTENING IN

X. ILLUMINATION AND BLINDING

XI. THE BELUMMATI CANTATAS

XII. UNBIDDEN I TURN

PREFACE

Divided into discrete sections like the months of the year or signs of the zodiac—and teeming with grief and wonder—Mackie Blanton's burgeoning collection of poems gathers the work of a rich lifetime. Among the many eclectic muses presiding over these poems, surely the most prominent is Hypatia, the Greek Neoplatonist philosopher and astronomer, worldly wise beyond her time, tolerant of diverse spirits and faiths, and empowered to reconcile those divided – she for whom "curiosity is sweeter / Than knowledge" so that, as Blanton imagines her, she chooses to "be devoured by / The quest of the unfamiliar / The unreliable, / The enduring." This ambitious quest carries Blanton across continents, as well as across history, cultures, races, and religions in a panoramic sweep of encounters, both literal and illusionary, that tease the senses and test the intellect. Line by line, moment by moment, page by page, each poem drops us, *kerplunk!*, in the middle of a strange setting (be it a café in Izmir or the swamps outside Chalmette, a small room in Paris by a flower stand or the sand dunes of Morocco), but always to trace the poet's thinking process in response to experience.

Whether writing of the impact of war in Rwanda where "there is no distinction between soldier / and civilian in the human hunt" or of a red ant that bites the poet's hand on his way to the mailbox, of the empty faith of a Vladimir Putin or of the figure of the poet's father, "cast in the sweet aroma / Of sweat, sawdust, and factory concrete floors," who "Like me, and now you, / …seemed to keep secrets," whatever comes into Blanton's purview triggers his thought toward not simply wisdom, but "the earthquake molecules of truth." "All windows are mine," he insists, "portals where all things / might be expanding." Yet despite his keen observations, he recognizes that "we cannot divine / with illusionary eyes" alone, without the mind's intricate leaps and bounds intervening, so that "illusion might transform our seeing." Akin to his poem in Hypatia's voice, this volume affirms how "A good book unexpected / Found is never a completion . . . / . . . but an unconscious, elated continuation / Of the life / Of the mind," as Blanton's "syllables and sentences. . .reach out / Toward galaxies" to offer us "A mosaic of the brain." Indeed, *The Casual Presence of Borders* may well be read as an almanac for consciousness itself.

—John Gery, author of *A Gallery of Ghosts* and *Have at You Now!*

I. A FAREWELL TO HINTS

THE SACRIFICE OF OUTCOMES

May I exceed my limitations and your understanding
To reassure you that history does not exist without wars,
Nor the sacrifice of outcomes? I am surprised that the few
Paragraphs I sent you from Knossos have stuck to my palms
Over all of these years. Now, here in Konya, I turn back
To them easily, page after page. There is nothing more
Than years than centuries. Being in the world provokes.

The diary is much dogeared, bound by Ethiopic leather
From the lower valley of the Omo River as a Sacred
Holy Text Aramaic tethered. An occasional blind
Finger mars the margins still, caressing every Syriac
Breath and syllable going off on its own. We often
Borrow our happiness from our imagined destiny
And it has all but evaporated by the time we emerge
Anew somewhere in a dream of being in the world

As a Recitation in a distant future. I have always preferred
To deflect my own edginess. The voices of my memories
And of my made-up stories are the hollowed-out murmurs
Of prison floors and endless dark tunnels, or corridors where
The chilled evening flinches into colder nights. The casual
Presence of borders are everywhere. All like the moon

Reflect actions at a distance in a world without evidence.
What is your ritual this century? Whom do you worship
On furlough; on forlorn, florid festivals and feasts these
Seasons, with or without
Reasons?
Who
Will die this year? Do we remember?
Perhaps I should ask
In September.
Let it rest as

The center arcs out as frontiers

Dissolving borders.

Then moves on
Over vagrant horizons.

In our remaining handful of days.
Do not scrape away the blood
From my crusted deserted tongue.
      Crack my throat
      So that I may use
      The rasp more
Pointedly,
And lose
      It by will when I need to.
The handheld soul of my soul is a restless censer.

I SWALLOWED A RED REFLECTION ENRICHED

Among unreadable faces at many banquets,
I once swallowed a celebration napkin's
Embroidered periphery's emboldened border's
Red reflection enriched edging down along
Cold decanted Death's Door gin, neat, of my cocktail glass.
      I faded into the wall,
      Unfaltering, slipping
      Away in my mind in a swirlwind
      Of fragrances and perfumes toward
      Anatolia, Lamu, Djerba, Fez, and
      Marrakech as a
      Massive irritable, spiteful
      Disturbance riffed about
      The air in the white lit hall.
If it isn't one thing, it's another, as my Mother
Always said, when she wasn't quite sure I was
Nothing like those others.
      I'll tell you no lies. Have you noticed
      I never respond to questions seeking
      Answers, for answers are there already,
      Upright ready, in the text and in you.
      You always ask what you already know.
      I want from you
Questions invoking responses, not answers,
Questions reaching in, ripping open, pulling
Out the future from the gut, grit, and guts
Of our seeking through flowing unfolding
Pages of our history and stories.
      Though you may not put words or
      Thought to what you were witnessing,
      You noticed, too, didn't you, feral Haman
      Dressed the part of an Afrikaner apartheid
      Strut, salivating at the border of Mexico:
      An unkempt suicidal unartful Patrician
      Pushing his latest deal: a breeding misogynist
      Sneak, a bleeder of wrong turns, surrounded
      By sycophants, hordes of phantom interns, refugees;
      Imagined migrant drug dealers, rapists; as he stiffened

There inside wrinkled khakis, eager to depart:
Amoral reflexes, a redundant, small, smallminded
Vocabulary tucked in hidden against his waist;
A stumped by life stumping conflict of selfdealing
Greed and grift. Did you spot the walled up
Expressions on military faces close by, edging
At the camera's angle? Each major
Disaster pushes us off toward the brink
Of boundary breaking destruction as it
Fizzles into a minor episode one after
The other as Haman's ordained
Authority.

Of course, literature needn't be factually true. True.
If it is, it's journalism, history, or sociology, which
Is how historians and cultural studies push it. For

Photojournalism breaks through.
Form follows function, they say.
Function is a need incarnate.
From my own angled illusion
Evil is as Evil does. Evil dies
As Evil lives.

I don't understand any of it, either,
Neither a non- nor un- American,
I do not grasp, get, clutch to my
Heart a trapped attention to commit
To intervention in nations of tribal
Nation States.

I dream, I hunger,
I ache for a New
World rainbow, never again enslaved
To European agas and ayahs toward
Whom priests, imams, rabbis once
Aimed, fired off, canons of sacred libido.

Before a thought comes to me,
I am not conscious of it. Then
Suddenly it's here. My thinking
About it becomes conscious, no
Matter how trivial or vital a thought
It may be. In this case, the thought
Is not conscious, but thinking,
Ruminating, rummaging, are.

What exactly does a written utterance
Mean? Does it mean that the thinker is
Not conscious of thought, as I have just
Suggested or does it mean the thought
Itself is not conscious ever of itself nor
Of the thinker to whom it enters in as
Intuition's instinct?

In the end, at the beginning: Antisemitism
Like racism or homophobia can neither be
Understood nor explained. It is just here,
Nurtured behind the brain blood barrier crossing,
In one's childhood household, as smug hatred
Resents Amharas, Armenians, Berbers,
Blacks, Browns, Eritreans, Habeshas, Hazaras, Kurds;
Countless ethnicities in diaspora within their own
Ancestral homelands and Stans, as are First Nations in,
Not of, the Americas, the Balkans, and Asia Minor.

Will we ever recognize
Our evil to correct it?
Why do we have this urgent instinct to divine
Enemies? Why is it that those who surmise
Weakness see hate and guilt in those they despise?
Why do we hate? Am I so innocent?
Well spoken and smart, some say
Of daily arguments against sociopathic
Amoral governments led by pathological
Liars. They are right, but my mind worries
More over those who read splenetic articles
In free countries and yet do not see or hear
Themselves in the negative frames of wishing
To drown journalists in blood of flames.

What would I say to a monstrous leader?
On the verge and edge of saying
This piffle or that bilge makes no
Sense to me? Hogwash discourse I
Realize neither evokes nor invokes
Common sense. Does it? Your crap
Makes us feel as if we are mired in
A rigmarole of mud and muck of our

Past all over again. Your own waves
Of disgust, regurgitated daily drivel,
Close in on you. Now alert, we return
To work to complete our projects of
Rebellion.
           Truth no longer has authority here.
           So be it! Unlike Haman, for whom
           It is always the color of skin that is
           In the game, we accept no promise
           Nor leers and lies from a soviet!
           But for the reverberating
           Echoes of his bile, why would
           Women of color, Christian and Muslim,
           Imitate their quaking men and throw shade
           Over, and shun, Jewesses desiring to march
                    With them?
Women marching after the vesselbreaking
Garden's Fall are One encompassing All.

SPIDERS AMONG SAGES

We each need to have and to own our own
Narrative. No one must own us this next time
In this struggle for wise equilibrium that we
Have come this far to meditate on, needing
No moneyed, altruistic landlords, overseers, or
Crackers with whips, nor where only scatter is·
Presence. Can we achieve this without turning
Back on Mankind, without lovers of the trite
Turning their backs on us? Who owns spite?

I used to imagine Africa's Augie of Hippo, Annaba's
Berber memory—restless backstreet rogue, rearguard
Churched Prince of self-denial, psychotherapy's first
Theological misogynist—relinquishing boyhood lust
And mayhem, for manhood's celibate Divine Love,
Puzzled by love, imagining his faithful:

> "Already they want me at Compline, below
> The Altar to imitate the far off Greeks whose
> Language I neither read nor speak. They wish
> To write an icon of me outside my cell inside
> An alcove niche in some square, quite close near
> My monastery. Or in the courtyard itself. They
> Think me a saint. I think they should draw there
> A Blue Jay instead, like my fatted, fated one I am
> Watching now beak breaking the earth for beetles,
> Seeds, or rotted, cast off figs.

> "I knelt at an open alcove as I first spotted my blue
> Jay's inn, a cracked, unused wooded cistern of straw.
> I squatted and slipped it young from its nest nestled
> There at the rim of its siblings waiting for their mother's
> Gliding back, with worms, I suppose. I am not caught
> And do not get pecked on about the head and neck all
> The way back to my cell. I feed it worms and sleep
> Along the rim of night."

Birds and worms. Worms and birds.

I imagine, too, Don Juan of Queens as Augie of Annaba
Before sainthood, before forgiveness, or the begging
For it, almost a stumbling saint arising. Without him,
America's vermin-infectious human boils would have
Remained below floorboards among spiders, hidden
From sages awakening among diffident birds of
Sainthood out of sight, late to take flight toward
Democracy's scattered presence.

Remapping influences, one may rethread alliances
Nonetheless as we in free fall veer toward a new era.
What have we been witnessing exactly? I have asked
Before: Were Osman, Cingöz Khan, Constantine,
Caesar, Alexander, David, Darius, Cyrus, different,
Much better? Has nothing changed the brain? Perhaps
The good a tyrant's daimon serves, if any at all, is
Afterwards, we can pick allies of a creed and breed
Broader, more diverse, from a swath of civilizations
With whom we might side by side, slide by slide, pride
By pride evolve ever more in a world where there is a
Forgiving time without tenses in tension. (But religions
Must not impede.) Where are the chirping, cheeping young
Who alone will ever truly know or, let alone, truly explore
The heart of another?

PRINCIPIA

Harvesting the stars' chemistry, conniving
Toward desire and escape, safe among

Fallopian entanglements, tethered
At the disorders of the umbilicus,

Our first hanging rope, between
The broken and the beautiful

Between mercy, duty, glory,
Then, then reason of a sort,

Here we are, at the very match
And matchmaking of the gears

And gong of our brain
In the universe's groggy

Galaxy of years: Youth
A newly emerging

Curse and culture of violence
And the first idols for worshiping

For eons to come in silence
The mind's inventions, the body's

Hungers and hangovers, when the buddies
Of molecules and atoms gangbanged us

Into the merciful and merciless deed
Of language to look up and proceed

Into the maw of wistful, wishful longing.

ALTOGETHER, ALL TOGETHER

Because we do not know
Because some refuse to lie
To themselves about that
Between the shadow and the silence,
Amidst the unordered order of voices,
I went off when I went away in my mind
To purchase common sense among buried
Rosetta stones among the ant-infested dust
Beneath the back porch of the wooded home
Of my youth. From the time I could be left alone.

Altogether a suicidal species against
Itself, we need rockets bursting through
Space from far off war-smitten galaxies
To pull us all together.

We should realize that when that happens,
We will soon be fighting our descendants who
Went off to colonize unknown planets and now
Want them for their own, and will strike
        A revolution to hold on.
        And strike a Constitution.

I knew nothing of nothing
And will never arrive, never get there,
As long as I do it right.
From the shore I depart to the horizon
Always there, seaweed steady,
        Coral reef sharp.
        Oyster reef ready.
My youth was a canvas unstretched,
Words unhammered by hands unformed.
But I knew the shape of desire all night long,
The promise of a rich interior life of dreams.

A lassitude in my gut now I watch news
Daily of worldwide gangbanger
Rapes, police brutality in God's name,

Earthquakes, plane crashes,
Forest fires, mudslides, hurricanes,
A moody tsunami bursting
Open smiles, doors, windows, drowning
The miserable asunder
In their underground storm cellars and brains.
How can we stomach so
Much old news anew all the days of our
       Lives?

When I look into the face of chaos, it is
As if it has no eyes
But when I get in closer, I see the eyes
Are slits, to let some
Light out and some light not
       Get in.

The face is there, smiling
Just above your head, even in the dark of night.
The light that gets through
Scrawls lewd, lurid graffiti on every wall we
Glide past, unknowingly blind
To the scratched, carved commands that bind
Our cheeks to the bark of trees,
Our feet to the rim of manholes we stumble to.
Here I sit. Here I stand. Here
I kneel to the soft flesh of day, the firm
Pillow of night: to the flesh
And pillow we call work, war, corruption,
Science, havoc, treachery, faith,
Money, films, coffee, to hand out or to take.
What's piking down the road for us,
       I'd like to know.

      Be careful of who
Smiles all the time, all the time, for they,
For they are suicides come with pikes
And pitchforks; and armed disarming
Sentences. They are graceful, autonomic
       Beasts.

Between the shadows and the silences,
Amidst the order of unordered voices,
I went away when I went off in my mind.
I knew nothing of nothing and nothing
Came in upon itself to continue my day.

LOGOCEUTICALS

Many sons of women have said
          In my father's house
          Are many mansions.
Many daughters of women have said
          In my father's galaxy
          Are many solar systems.
But many religious sons of men and women change
The vocabulary. What we once knew as university
Textbooks we now call rental texts and buy-back books.
Indifference occupies the trammeled territories of intellect.

In brilliantly lit sleights of memory, I hunt exact words
To swallow, to capture meaning alive. I continue sifting
Syllables for the correct logoceuticals but the wraith winds
          Of wrath lift them away.

These daily or yearly devotions are my only therapy.
They slip from me slowly at my desk. I am the dog
On the front lawn whose agitated bowels move out
Like time crystallizing, fragmenting, fracking,
Into the grass. Does one notice?

As a child I soon calculated that I could measure
Dignified destitution by the length of a man's belt,
Bigger than his waist, hanging below, or fitted all
The way around to a last shapeless loop behind
His hip. A fatted banker's belly's belt was almost
Too small to buckle, heaving below duped cigar
Breathlessness and wheezing.

I learned to chat with manipulation with those who bore
Watching, as if my eyes laced around by Titus' Arch
Loomed high above my head.

Sinister questioners abound. Of Jews, they say self-hating;
Shame and self-loathing of Blacks, they say. I say it is not
Tribes but civilizations of blood that are in diaspora millions
Upon millions of centuries. I have bitten into the American Dream.

My gums bleed every moment the Dream refuses to give, then turns
Aside my awakening on my own terms:
>To join and seal with the haste
>And the taste of blood my identity
>In events at once unique and indistinguishable
>In composition, control, and secrecy; in turbulence and
>>uncertainty.
We all of us are the mothers of the daughters and sons of women
and men.

MEMORY BEING NOT VERBATIM

What are we doing here?

To be, who are we being here?
What happens in conversations,
          What some call
                    Discourse,
          Or nothing at all,
          Happens when with neither aim
          Nor target, lame
                    Discussions ensue
                    And coiled memory
          Not always precise,
          Being not verbatim,
          Is not reliable unknotted.

Who recalls the origin, grown together,
Of spacecraft Cyprus settling below the belly
Of shadowing Asia Minor?
Or of Crete, anvil to the gods,
Floating below, beyond, Lesbos?
Only books leathered with dust do.
To be, what are we doing here?
What are we not doing here?
Against one another,
                    Lives
Are in service
          To incestuous hives
Cloning
          Separate
          Enslavement camps, cliques, and rookeries.

FRANÇOIS VILLION EASTWARD DOWNRIVER

I must step into and cross territories that I do not know
And not be confused, nor disturbed, by the shadow of a
Hawk swooping through, nor the smooth flow of flutes,
Nor the driving drones of hirsute nuns and hoary lutes.
My reach is my power, not my god or my guide, as I earn
My keep. What we believe limits what we know. I want
Out. I don't want to be disappearing, nor dying with
Expectations. So much depends on being found centuries
Off, decades away. Cities here will drown in denial, from
Thunderous rains, rising floods, plunging bombs, rising
Graves. Award me with the alpha female wolf to lead me
To my Anatolia. I'm learning lately trust means having
Expectations, and having expectations means I'm not
Fully here, imperceptibly there, nor completely free.

MULATTO, JULATTO

At the gate of the city that matters,
Houses angled like wedges of nuptial
Cake toward Mid City boulevards and streets,
Rests a plaque that reads
          The Only City That Matters.
Africa's ghosts, spirits, and music matter.

Plaque on the gums,
Of Corpus Americanus,
Plaque inside the channel of arteries
And carotids where the id rots first,
          Narrows the slide of
          Blood flow. For generations matter
Exactly where we dwell once again, now again,
And again now to quell the skull's riot of nerves
In this city as caring and mattering remembers
History's victims' inescapable painful proofs,
Not disunion's ideology's peace-muffled assertions?

The essential human being is a ghost
Swirling among an air of ghosts.
How might we identify one another?
          Mulatto, Julatto?
          Ugandan Jew?
Greek Turk, Turkish Greek?
Iraqi Kurdish Jew, Jewish Iraqi Kurd?
American Black, Black American?
          American African?
Arab Christian, Christian Arab?
Jewish Arab, Arab Jew?
Arab Muslim, Muslim Arab?
Greek American, American Greek?
Armenian Turk, Turkish Armenian?
Turkish American, American Turk?
          Croatian Persian American?
          Jewish Ethiopian?
          Irish Serbian Jew?
                    You, too!

Who matters?
All lives matter, they say.
Black Lives, Brown Lives,
White Lives, Red Lives,
Yellow Lives.
But herein lies the beast:
Whom we see who matters least.

RIB CAGE AND BACKBONE

I do not intend to leave behind a record of my
          Ambivalent deliberations.
An ordinary stretch of time, death, a fierce
Smell under my nose all night, all day, may
Come in an hour or in any hour in any year away.
I imagine you notice the menacing, mincing aging I hide.
          Your new husband has remarked
          On my right leg limping.
It's also in your mother's stride.
An unfamiliar pain is always new and noticeable.
My avoidances unfixed by words are thoughtless,
Clueless minced prayers in an off night to our
DivineHoly Something or Other for those who wish
          To live in a world without evidence.
                    What if it isn't true?
                    None of it?
The drama of identity and modern desires seek a now,
          Hardly ever a here.
Here can be anywhere. Now is everywhere all the time.
          The calling of questions, a law
          Of bee fever in mosaic, gnaw
          At my vertebrae and ribs.

TAKING THE MEASURE OF A SPLIT SECOND

By daybreak, white tiger bearish clouds muffle darkening thunder
By dusk. Through a moonlit pellucid sky's blunder, earsplitting
Lightning crack all week. Downpours insist flash floods down
Every drain hole, imprinting a granular sheath over the amygdala
Of a generation. I once wondered often why we come here, why
We sputter out storms of reasons for doing something, anything,
Or nothing at all, here, and now understand that we are here as
Spotlights seeking attention. No matter where we are, in any
Neighborhood, town, city or mountain slope, or nearby prairie
Or swamp, no matter how insignificant a human thing we may be,
Our Eastern mystical or Western analytical or ancient Africana
Selves are noticed or ignored, each at a startled or stared attention.

Behind Harvey, as we now already know, were Irma, Jose, Katia,
And Michael. So quick to arise and bear down so close, there may
Be at least four more over the next two months before the hurricane
Disaster season subsides into its annual calendar silence. Hurricanes
Remind me, sardonically, as I've noted before, of the separate but
Equal Turkic tribes hoofing across the Caucasian Steppes into eleventh
Century Asia Minor, all the while glancing over their shoulder, gazing
Cautiously back behind lest they be overtaken by an offending brethren
Tribe. That bookish image makes me realize that the modern West
And Eastern Europe haven't changed all that much. In a world where
What we believe limits what we know, we join ourselves to nature's
Slaughter and the putdown of others. Our brain causing experiences,
Mediates, meditating and mediating the curve of grief and symmetry.
   Leaving not behind even those who believe
     There is no world to come, no afterlife,
       Can we get back the past
       To the very split second before
       Forgetting a life in space and time
        We as energy and matter
         Slipped
         Here now,
         There then,
          Into
          Borders?

MYTH, ANTHEM, MEMORY

In the Days of Heat and Horse, when all
But a few were too poor for peace of mind,
When the price of resistance or mere truculence,
If not death sourtasting on the tongue, was exile
   Or imprisonment
   Or confiscation
     Of goods, women, and children
   Or slavery.
One had to beseech rather than demand, beg
Rather than insist. We know we are strangers
Or outsiders who have come here before. What
If we stop right here for a while, then move on,
Leaving behind in the dust and debris from an
Encampment food scraps, broken dishes and bones,
Or fading on walls
   Prints of ritual on bended knees,
   Bowed foreheads, and supplicant palms?
Should I strike a scene? How should I direct?
   Open wide the casements
   Of human consciousness?
Broaden the borders of human understanding
And the nature of knowledge? Some of us are
   Already down to the short rows
With our cameras above our heads in the clouds.
Ready to shoot, edit, comment, and blog.
   We are
   Myth, Anthem, and Memory.
Sportsmanship is instant replay in the moment.
Foreplay delays the thrill, no longer bringing joy,
   Nor ecstasy.
   We are
Dealers and brokers in—what is the phrase?—Pale
   Pain and Human Tragedy.
   Bring us more stories.
   Sometimes we just lie,
   Mehmet Bey.
There are still more codes to break our back to crack.

As it happens, stories and storytelling, as Plato says
Of all true philosophy, are preparations for dying.
Stories, as it so happens, even when false are true.
Here, let me help you. You might skid on these
Slippery stone slopes uphill. I do not want you in a
Coma for the rest of my life. An addiction to one's
Flaws can be one's purpose in life. This changes
Everything. Though easy to see the sky from the sky,
It is difficult to see the world from the world. Why
In nursing homes do patient inmates have no autonomy?
Robotomatonic inmates they become. Religion eases their
Pain: it makes sense of what makes no sense about the world.

How is your Grandmother, Mehdi Bey?
How often do you get to Kuşadası?
Do you still collect the monthly rent
For your Father in Basmane?

When will Turkey and America become twin Nations
Of Democracy, left alone by Russia, and leave alone
Exactly where their history and art emerged and lie

And still thrive:
Greece

And leave alone comely
Thessaly,

Where Atatürk matured, and who wishes only to endure?

ONKELOS ON THE LAW OF INVARIABLE UNORDER

Obsession entwined arising
                    At birth with the child's brain,
Wrongly diagnosed, is not
                    A disorder, but the mind's banked
Phenomenon, a paradigm,
                    Of unchaotic unorder; a complexity
And uncertainty; a remarkably
                    Predictable, deterministic
Reduction in complications:
                    A simplicity of its own constant
Or variable magnitude.
                    Each baby a miracle before
The hugs, kisses, and squeezes
                    Of 'rents and 'sins, tossed
Asunder, take over. When will
                    The child in Manhood and
Womanhood break? Never as
                    Long as Hagar and Sarah
Lilith and Chava
                    Wander in the Deserts
Of consent of Beersheba
                    Of Paran.

THE PLANT PRINCIPLE

Time has come, we have chosen,
My wind will no longer shake
Your blood to fall in petals,
But to subsurface and to slowripple
As oceansea harbored at your horizon
Of bone, for we came to giftstill your
Monthly waves, to embroidered
There with seeded timewebbing
A ninemonth solitaire.

We will soon know of life
As we know of one's death
In our sometimes attempt
That rooted within seconds
To spread across our roof
And sprout not and coil not
The hospital ward into a parlor.

An unknown body lies now
Beneath your garden, veining
The brilliance and the agony
Of your earth. She will dress herself
In darkness for now to go down
To the slope of your city, where
The heat from your gated loins
Wrapped in this land's dimestore
Cotton, reminding me of the undershirts
I have abandoned or of the tablecloth
I am endeared to, will be a breeze
Of nursing hands. We have not been
False to this pearly talent of thought
Endowed in our groins. We have taught,
Taught your dress how not to wrinkle
But to ruffle up, or my hands how
To accept the handful bearing of your mind.

NEED

I am feeling more and more like an inmate these days.
What do we need more, drama or transport; words
Shadowfisting frustration in the air or silence as
The lunar moon shuttlecocks into view against
A salmon, softened twilight?
          Books will lose that new book smell we sense
          As their perfume, their fragrance. New books
          Burnished at some point in the future we will
          Call multidimensional hypertexts. Imagine
          Résumés and artists' portfolios as simultaneous
          Audio, video, and manuscript hyperpropriocepts.

What are we a stereotype of? I cannot even imagine.
At these crowded hours, first things first. Imagine
The prow and the rudder keeping distances apart.
Imagine on a clear day a home appraiser and inspector
Letting more sunlight in from attic to basement.
We look and do not see, hear and do not listen, as
We were told uncountable billions of waves over
Spume ago. Sometimes there is even the supercilious
Sniff as I, clothed in spoiled arrogance and steely
Insouciance, walk past severely creased khaki chinos.
Why not? To whom do I owe what? Very little moves
Me more than object-oriented language, an array of
Suffixes, sentence-converted desire, predicate trees,
Lattices of infixes, verbs of destiny, deed, and will.
Imagine this: the superior camouflaged nightjar
Whippoorwill late evenings and early mornings
Challenging the misfit limitations of human beings.

.

II. GOING OUT, COMING IN

BLIND FIBER

The blizzard had not gone away.
To stack back the hours of paper
trays and words, we entered
                an Olde Towne café;
because it is sad to turn a chill
grimace to the Chicago air or claw
at the snow that packs back our
homestead toil and blisters our
days over the soil of spoils.

There
perched like a queenfisher crane:
nightlife's storyseer, her brain
in song, upon her barstool. She
dwelt upon the light, confined,
shut in by edges' tight shapes,
to an endless beam of day in,
day out, as if trapped there
in the middle of a centerless
Great Books discussion where
the dismal, scattered room
suggests a university's bigotry
                of low expectations

                and I, you: two grains among
                the shadowwall of listeners
                in the sun square, knew then
                there must be
                                a gentler word
about death
                                the striking
glittering cord   that necklaces
the throat with tightening tenderness
                                that caresses the hands
and feet with binding, blinding dominion
                                that shrouds up colors
of your dress and my suit into a single, stiff matter,
                a word

about death
              the bodyact
that shuts out   the mind's lastnext recall,
              a silk rockword
that cords the unraveling beads of breath
that threads and stitches the needle
              back
into the tailor's pocketpalm.

She dwelt upon our public minds,
latticed and trellised by faces
              eyeing the Blues,
converging in a stillness
of smiles and watchfulness.

                    And I knew,
Consciousness from matter, provoked by doubt,
had come aboutface, that she had no use for us,
that it was all of a piece,
that it was a day without yesterday,
that she had entered Vietnam's ardent, unvisited city
              in song,
        blood's memorial body,
                    and spread her sunblooming skin
                    across America's lawn of gates,
this BlueEyedBlackAmericanAsian child of war,
                    and cast the shade of trees
                    down among the glades where
                    warriors of grass, longer nothing,
        gnarl up dormant and extravagant
              in anthems.
The city is a piece, we are a piece, threading
under and are caught up for a century or more,
on a single danger night of despair and lore;
contradictions of alienation and conversion,
cloaked and canopied by riots in the streets,
secret shuffling by overlords scrambling,
bodyslamming universities against graystone,
redbrick, and slavewrought iron pikes.

She nonetheless
preferred to overwhelm
        in
    as we ambled
        out.

SEEKING A METASACRITURE

What's remarkable about unsocial philosophers
Today is that most of them hold forth as if they
Are still in training to disbelieve in Sanghas, Shuls,
Chapels, and Mosques: an irony, you see, about
These whose favorite opprobrium is "Counterintuitive!"
When stomping ass backwards, glass of wine or gin
In hand, to break into serious conversations of others
At cross purposes who nonetheless seek mystical
Understanding of how being uncertain of anything works.
       These are days when most Americans
       Keypad curate their daily identities
       In a bubble of passivity for just being.
       No wonder it is the philosopher's task
       In museum gatherings to jerk our attention
       Around to the fact that in such freedom
       To be whoever we wish to be, to think
       Whatever we wish not to believe, we are
       Mostly illogical if not irrational. It's a matter
       Of rational research, I suppose, to discern who
       Really is in training.
As I recognize a category of believers by what
Verses they never evoke, I recognize philosophers
By questions they never offer. Doubt and questions
Are forms of worship. That is how I worship, at any
Rate. Except to a few historians of mind, the question
Is of no importance. We pursue truth where we live.
A bit of cutthroat reflection is necessary. Why else
Would I embarrass myself here in front of *you*
By searching for, seeking, a metasacriture
That recreates, envelops, and evolves us
And not need a metaphysics of being,
         Nor of not-being?
         Nor of non-being.
       It is not clever to hate even as we hate cleverly.
       Tears along the cheeks of our innocence,
       An inheritance without hatred these days,
       I prefer (and hope you do also); and prefer
       Leaving the room without explanation,

Imagining I have taken the conversation
With me out through the window,
             Hand in hand,
             Heart to Heart,
And the room had fallen into silence.
Perhaps because behind those walls
Upon walls of talk, merely talk, are
Persons who think themselves to be agents
Of the Spirit, of the unseen transcendent
Suggestion in the gray air shocking allegiances
And assurances from our choking throats.
If I keep up their conversation in my head, ants
Scraping their way up through my eyes, I,
A fugitive without identities, engaging a
A stranger, myself, I learn more about
Myself and what I really think of war,
Of faith, the future, of putting up with new
Births on this planet. My thoughts always
Peter out the same way: my wondering
How we could possibly justify our shameless
Existence and insistent presence in this solar
System. For not even the galaxy is expansive
             Enough to hide us.
                   So
I read all sides to know who draws lines, carves out borders,
             To learn where and how lines and borders are drawn.
             Evolution shapes us over time toward
             Ways we may survive. A village, town,
             City, country, or nation never leaves us
             Alone. We have got to find the middle way.

FOR WE DIE

> Americans desire to rediscover that
> What we call religion matters.

True, lives matter.

> What we call race matters.

Truer even: Both misnomers,
> Race and Religion,
> Yoked skin and blood,

Matter. Boundary to boundary. Border to border.
> Blood to blood.

So much pitter, patter, tatter, matter
> That we the worldover pit groups against

One another because such groups the worldover
Matter against
> One another to matter
> Moreso over

Matter,
> Since the beginningless beginning.

Just how do we identify?
> Senegalese American? American Senegalese?
> > You know what I mean,
> > If you please.

> Arab Muslim? Muslim Arab?
> Greek American? American Greek?
> > You there, you know
> > What I mean. Speak
> > > Up!
> Armenian Turk? Turkish Armenian?
> Native American? First People American?
> > Mixed? Miscegenated?
> > > America?

American Indians Matter! Mexican Americans Matter!
Cuban Americans! Honduran Americans! Cajun Americans!

Where is the Catalan? The Basque? The Berber?
> The Yoruba, Kashmiri, and Kurd?
In all of this matter; in all of this that matters?

Not a group,
Only the individual,
        I here proclaim,
Can bring about change,
        But never will, for we die one
By one
            As a group and as one,
            Though we are the blame
                    And the same
                    As the borders of cells
                    Shrivel up.
                    Why do you gulp,
                    Swallow, guffaw?
Do not argue that this is a banal conservation of guesses
For all serious discourse, discussion, and conversation
                    Are internal.

AMONG TRANSLATORS

I wander at a slant among Rabbis, Imams, and Orthodox
Priests. Pretending that I do not know what they would
Want of me, I wonder, "What is it they want of us?" I
Do not wish their certainty without insularity, and hurry
Along outside of their fixed-footed distance. I therefore
Reside and sleep sometimes even among their texts,
In the comfort of words conversing in my brain in many
Languages in translation.

Somehow somewhat somewhere, we are redrawing maps
But I cannot yet tell which empires are ending. Chaos
Is still King or Queen. I have dreams that my body takes
A break to pee and I cannot fit the pieces back together.
I lie there listening to the clocks chime and ping the time
Seconds, often minutes, from one another. The keywound
Grandfather is often behind. I have no patience with it. It
Was there in my childhood home before I entered it at
Birth. It was there ambient in the living room off from
The room of my first crib dreams. I grew up rewinding
Those ornate brass plated Roman numerals until the day
I left home for unknown worlds. It chimes and tick-tocks
Ubiquitous in my head always.

Whose name known among us is not a supreme example
Of the advantages and disadvantages of mystical celebrity?
Common facts among them is that many greats have produced
Along the way probing texts both of oblique and blinding
Brightness. Yet, devoted to falsifying fame, the non-devotional
Media and fans not necessarily worthy of an opinion will under
Imagined duress always shout, "One of America's
Greatest *this*, *that* or *the other!*" Or "The best of
His or Her generation!" Value is given nowadays
Not by voracious students beforehand, nor quiet,
Unknown readers, to any piece in the market place
More than only fingering intrinsic worth as afterbirth.

We no longer decide value by ourselves.
Perhaps we hardly ever have.

THE CLOSING

Why has the planet been so cursed with autocracy?
Is it that we, permanently startled into complicity,
Only sit and stare? Have we no revolutionary heart?
Does it really matter, as my friends of, supposedly, higher
Consciousness maintain? A Messiah's suffering, after all,
Teaches us: *We give in in order to get our own way*.
       Sacrifice is the game's
       Medal to pin on.
For all we know, our idiots may be our messiahs.
       Nothing to lose, actually,
       Below or above.
       The pout and pettiness of
The millers, the banners, the trumpeters, all mere
Rebirths again and again and again from
Our bowels, mouths, nostrils, and ears, err
In our time, during their vulva-fiddling crossing,
       Engulfed
      By a frieze of poems
        Yet unsung,
        Yet unnarrated.

The future comes on at the rear, nomadic
Tribes arising from the silk sand of the moon,
Galloping on astride small steeds from
Parental steppes familial. Furtive horsemen
Warriors glance back in trained formation
Over their shoulders, right, left, ahead,
Behind, discerning unfamiliar flags among
The suffering of women to come.

Closing on. In the blood.
Closing in. On the blood.

Not men without flaws, yet
Drawn through resistance
Toward the monarch's mind
Dwelling in every human brain;
Aware, off course, of the betrayers

Swamped under accessible flaws,
Enslaved in the very heart and spirit
Of slave owners—our Washingtons,
Jeffersons, Madisons, Hamiltons, who
Recreated us nonetheless to notice
        With suspicion
Monarchical Georges, Caesars, Sultans among us
With the lens and gaze, the garment
And cloak, of a Constitution, Flag, a
Declaration against eternal enslavement.
        We had nothing to lose,
         A vision to inhabit.
The patient guiddle player, not yet ready
Even to rehearse, practices a republic
Of verses, a civilization of myths
Traced in the borders of blood, amidst
An apprehensible truculent breeze
        At our dry lips.

CHOICE AND TURTLES

I of a morning at times have the feeling
I will wake up invigorated, refreshed,
Pulling myself from beneath the blankets,
Lifting up relaxed at the edge of the bed;
Stretch without yawns and rise energetic
To walk toward the bedroom doorway hall
Leading to the kitchen to prepare the morning
Coffee, as usual. I look back at my wife and see
                    Still there
                    Me beside her.

I am having this vision now, in the passenger
Seat on a warm, sunny midmorning promised
Rain as we motor South, as usual, along America's
Longest bridge across a lake, my wife at the wheel,
Ever closer to the City. North behind us now,
The clouds still opaque overhead, now toward
Translucent South, waterboard the New
Orleans Horizon.

The way the worlds focus in we cannot divine
With illusionary eyes unless, caught up by
Surprise, we defocus out. Choice and turtles
All the way down: of parents, mates, form,
And dirt. We each, the least measured thing
That can happen, jump into unmeasured
Momentum and position, the plenitude
Of reality invisible on every immeasurable human shelf.

INTERSTICES

Our brain—our body's substrate basilica
Of all feeling and thought, of human

Energies shoulder to shoulder, of endless
Self-chat, gossip, and boasting we call prayer,

Ritual, and redemption; of problems with
The fragmented Self, tiled in ribbons

Of perpetual grimaced grins, through whose
Veins and arteries flows a fourth of the body's

Blood—creates the vulgarity and beauty of love
And war, assessing despair, desire, fear, pity,

Anxiety, potency and impotence; the lies, myths,
And imaginings of narrative memory; passion,

Compassion, and detachment, interlayered agency
Interlaced with all the spirits of eons where

Our sacred neurotic selves praise in hosannas
Any deity or idol we choose to bow before.

Beyond all the brains across the planet are forces
And images of innocence, uncertainty, trauma,

And healing of even one brain, in its recondite, forlorn
Enskulled Caprice Incarnate, and may have had nothing
            To do with any of it.
            By bit,
            It's all good.

I no longer choose. Being not even an Agnostic
At the Center allows me to learn without preamble,
Evaluation, and judgment. I don't care anymore
About What created What or What created Whom
            Or Who created What and Who.

It's myths and anthems all the way,
All the way up and all the way down,
Up and down; down and up and all
        Around:
        Inside out,
        Outside in.

TWILIGHT'S SPILLOVER

Twilight roars twice a day, descending.
On the battlefield where our mitigated,
Shifting selves abrade. The hippocampus
Welcoming new neurons every day, what
Exactly separates alone human experiences
Of misdirection and subterfuge, of love
And fear, upon stone, sand, and high waters,
Will I never discover? How universal
Are the human heart and soul? What do we
Know of the suffering of soldiers returned
And returning home? I must drink less
And exercise more.
        I am not alone. My eyes and those
        Of billions bleed ink, print,
        From books, texts, written and read
        About suspicion, mistrust, animosity,
        Friendships; as we ease daily down
        Into the sky's light between full night
        And sunrise and between
        Sunset, full night: a helping
        Light offered twice a true day,
        From sundown to sundown,
To all of us by the diffusion of sunlight's leer
Or airglow descending through an atmosphere
Of dust at its dawn and dusk.
I grieve
For my much-mistaken country
        As much as I would for any authentic
        Human genealogy's complexities
        Of centuries of human anxiety and fear,
        Of centuries of boundaries and borders.

Which of these peoples on the planet will protect
One another? Who will protect me? Why do these
Questions insist? Conspicuous is risky. Rumpled
Bastions of speech or trampled thinking ridiculed
Is safer, quickly unnoticeable.
Rats of isolation on tiptoe gather

At the heels and ankles
Of the unnoticed, biting
Into their flesh, crunching
Their bones, sucking their blood,
Crushing their spirit toward infirmity and dying.
The rats are forever, abandoning space only
To roaches. Unlike this or that people who
Seek revenge, I seek from the heart to rout
Out all haters who arouse their own heart's
Impotence; but realize then that my heart, too,
Is impotent under such seeking. Must I retreat
Then to indifference, to catatonic analysis
Of lost civilizations?
All stories buried alive are stored away
     As relics
     Of uncertainties.
Are our experiences choreographed
     Allegories?
Is what we perceive and believe
We feel *what actually is?*
What breathless single narrative,
     Embodied, clearing its throat
     Before entering,
     Wheezes behind the veil
     Of perception and uncertainty?
How can we unknow uncertainty and be free?
You don't know what
     I am thinking of, do you?
     I understand: none asks,
     What is he thinking *of?*
     They ask instead, What
     Is he saying? What
     Is he thinking? *Of*
     Fallen off the edge
     Does no longer exist
     Here.
You don't know, do you?
You don't remember
     Being there. What I want
     You to learn by unknowing

Is that no incarnation
Has ever failed here.
No incarnation is a failure,
Neither yours nor
My own. We were never dealt a hand.
We always play the role we chose
Beforehand, becoming and coming
Into view. Try to remember
It, insteeled in us,
This spillover.
Some of us are sprouts; others, lint,
On a green blanket
Pretending blue.

HUMOR PLANTED THERE

Language, a wily oboe smuggled down along our nervous
System beneath our brain, from stem to coccyx, from stem
To stern, can delay meaning, defer meaning, reverse meaning,
Stir new winged notes of meanings. A wonder instrument it is.
Without it, what choices have we? Not myth but the lack
Of it. Not ideals but the spread of greed and murder. Not
Irrepressible civility but abrasive oblivion. Not the creative
Impulse but the trample of revelations in perpetuity. Not
Immeasurable yearnings but the dampening of desire.
I have forever known males and females with dream skin:
Subtle natural flecks of gold, copper, reds, and amber
Glinting their black, dark brown, light brown, dusty,
Or white skin. I have always loved Louisiana faces
Because of these friends and schoolmates of my
Childhood. We bloomed together midcentury amid
An audacious, amorous, imperceptible New Orleans
Humor planted there by nuns, priests, parents, disk
Jockeys, Baptists, and breakups, or the occasional
Rabbi mind-melding profitable advice, caprice, family
Contradictions. Breakups cultivated us toward young
Adulthood, betrayals, and forgetfulness. Laughing,
I am pressed to engrave these faces here before our eyes
Because of the America that mauls our memory and future.
The more diverse we become bleeding out in an unscripted
World, the more segregated we become. Americans desire
Minorities, underdogs, and victims to forgive its battles
Against all notions undemocratic, unconstitutional,
And un-American: embossed synonyms that seduce
Or molest our vocabulary of liberty, freedom, and death.

COMING HOME

Years ago, sometime after relocating a homecoming from
Chicago to New Orleans, over a meal at the kitchen table,
We talking about nothing much at all, my wife for no reason
I can now recall, revealed that she began to have migraines
After she had married me. At the time, we had already been
Married for at least thirty years. Not after she married or after
We had married, but after she had married me. In the Ozarks,
In the NW corner of Arkansas, this resilient mountain princess
Who later would marry me had begun life doing the family
Ironing at the age of five, and running over snakes atop the
Family tractor a few years later. I have learned over the years
Not to stare wordshocked at her indirect or direct reprimands
But to slowly look up then off as if toward a relentless window,
Then to gaze toward her with soft contemplative eyes and
No-mind, and be a lighthouse upon her face. She is my constant
Shadow self and companion. As with our daughter, I learn a lot
About myself as I witness me in the two of them: one my heart;
The other, my heartbeat. I look, then see what I lack that they
Embody. They are my sun and moon warming toward the West;
Cooling from the East: the winter evening green of the tops of
Trees, Magnolias and Oaks, along the overshadowed roads home.

THE PLESSY FERGUSON OVERTURE

Never more than ever than right now,
                          We gamble a century on rhymes
On larger than life hide and go seek
                          Selfies dominating the lens
In front of monuments and countrysides,
                          Family and friends diminished
In the background. When those who
                          Stifle in place rule without
Thought wonder what it is to be human,
                          They seek contrition in metaphysics
And neuroscience. The beleaguered ones
                          Ramshack the arts for identity
And solace. Thought, endless and infinite,
                          Comes and goes as many measures
Whose totality is both lock and key. Yet each
                          Side blind in agony deafen the universe
Of laws. We cannot hear elusive reality chuckling with us.
                          Ridicule, a sucker punch to the throat
Of empathy, leads to hate, a smash to the face of love.

THERE SPEAKS MARTIN DE PORRES VELÁZQUEZ

Poor Fools. Forever destitute in spirit and body. At last implications
Are clear. Truly, the Black individual is not invisible. Never has been.
It's rather the rich or poor peckerwood cracker who is hiding beneath
A vote against his own best interest not to be imagined Black. I've
A cracked mirror across my face while I linger here. Where exactly
Am I imagining here whom I am observing there? Or do I observe
There whom I am imagining here in lopes and sways? I look. I watch.
I meditate. I contemplate. Colors and sounds alive taste sweet on my
Tongue as I gaze upon my two icons: Egypt's Joseph in his long rainbow
Waistcoat; Arimathea's Joseph of wealth and multiple burial caves
                    For Rabbis and Resurrections.

Where am I? Which basement? Which office? Which cell? Cell of which
Priory of which century? Which back porch? From which crib of memory,
                Reaching out to touch my grandmother's apron?

Mystics, madmen, their inconstant bewildering murmur of thought confound
The attributes of my heart. My dog, cat, bird, and mouse eat together with me
From one same dish as Crucifix and Rosary hang safe among the washed straw,
Cleansed daily, of my broom moping, leaning obediently nearby in the corner,
                    Alert.

FOOL'S GOLD

New York's whiny gold-chaired national child, now
Inaugurated, worrying us months ago, we have to pan
The stream, to sift out the dross, the stench of words and thought.
Magazine, stage, and tv satirists have trouble
Exaggerating Haman's id. He has diminished
Them, rendering their mirrored antics less credible, less creative,
Less comedic, as less real as Haman himself.
No matter what we watch or read, it's always
Haman's news. Is he doing this to us or are we doing this
To ourselves? By *this*, I mean no longer
Laughing, as we, our gall or joy bursting at the seams
Of intelligence, choke, guffaw, mock or praise him.

Our next new civic duty, to keep our eye on
The monkey-shine of the eunuch impulse in the House
And Senate, denies us the ease to become
Inured to the smirking, malignant shade
They drool. They bear more watching
Than Ham, who implodes every day, at times
Several times a day, with searing lies light itself,
Embarrassed, cannot ignore as reason, then looks
Away. His eunuchs explode
With the same agreed stick of dynamite
Up their diffident rectums each new
Morning to pose ahead of freedom and Ham
Himself. Soon Everyone will run over one
Another, I am convinced. We want
To be alert enough to witness
The unbearable ruins among monuments.
Ham has damaged his improbable
Statues in possible squares with social
Justice activists worldwide, with Democracy's
Intelligence; with China, with
Germany, with Iran. At some
Point Greece, Israel, Saudi Arabia, Britain,
And Turkey will push back against
The exaggerated inexplicable that will
Damage them. They will have no choice.

The stage is set,
The cable screens well lit.
Four-year old Ham pouts.
Saul, neither centurion nor saint,
Gaveling the House into Session,
Crosses himself. He will soon escape.
Impotent roaches grin and swarm.

Roach-ridden impotence swarms.
No doubt, "believers" who favor these
Shenanigans are unbelievers complicit in
Theological ignorance, political and
religious Corruption.

I should practice detachment.

We should watch though,
Never to turn away
Rehearsing America's Democracy
Narrative we imagine scripted across
The sky as we await the moment to
Practice, to replay. Our destiny will
Always lie in waiting, rehearsing,
Practicing, reliving.

SLOGGING TOWARD PERFECTION

Traumatic Stress, Disease, Disorder, Syndromes,
                However labeled, though
                I, anal, have no right to,
        Posted first class along the home
                Of nerves splintered
By shrapnel from a birth, a war, a parent's throat,
A teacher's inclined stare across the muddy moat
                Of the innocence
                Of flamed colored cloaks
Tied together by the tyrant of irrational bonds
                And shared mythic memory,
Something always sticks. So throw all myths and facts at
The wall to tear them down one day. Let's not let what
Slides to the floor slide off. Let's not sneak off to abandon
The stubborn stains refusing to dry there at the wall. They
Will be resuscitated until all myths and facts abandon one
Another for a free universe refusing to be buried by envy
And avarice for geography. Will no one regret some little
Thing, if not everything? Interpretation of narrative and
The universe sometimes backdoors into an arresting flow
And swirl over narrow canals; relying always on the ability,
                Toward shifts, of twists in Language.

NAKED HOMELANDERS

Is your mouth afraid of me,
My Country Tears of Thee?
Am I Meursault to you?

How will we ever understand and heal the victim
And practitioner of perfect oppression; the warrior
Home, the boat people of Vietnam or Cuba, the Central
City kids who murder one another, the reservation men
Who knead their fists into their women as easily as
Pounding millet; the Holocaust and Nakbah survivors
And the children of Survivors who are never calm,
                At home, or at ease except
                With each other somewhat?
We are all naked homelanders from a distant savannah
                Of suns and sunlit moons.
Though bruised by major aggressors and minor stereotypes,
We must name them all to transform the pervasive grieving.

I miss the old days of television when service was included
In the news we devoured, when news anchors' faces fronted
Toward the screen in clarity and downright alive authority;
Nothing at all like today's frenetic hosts, chests heaving, hands
And arms flailing to grasp meaning and meaningfulness, fumbling
Forward in shouts, in gasps, in spittle, breaking through, stumbling
Over to break into, to break apart ideas their invited guests, muffled,
        Swallowing hard, are invited to come up with
                Guffawing,
                Laughing.

Like cyber news bloggers, waiting, trending, transferring in, or
Like any novelist's last three years, all the while suffering from
Depression and addictions: writing for cable film studios,
Struggling financially to make ends meet, supporting a daughter
And son in private school and an estranged spouse's secret
                Sanatorium staycation.

They and their descendants generations to come will be perfectionists:
Born in anger, wedded in anger; give birth in anger, rearrange families
In anger. Nothing is ever right. We have no future, in truth.

In every second, our future is our past
                 With them, their kind.
                 We must work against
                 The consumerist geist,
                 Never make it easy for them
                 To figure out why we need
                 To test others' patience.
                          So be it.
                 I do not mean to be a pest,

                 Our Country, T'is of Thee.

THE COOP OF GOD

A distant inland wind
Has arrived, has aroused the dead,
Slumbered strengthening of the stoneslate walls.
                    On the bishop's palace algae
Has yellowed the green brick, deepened the red.
                    A cavernous, monkish silence braces
The halls. Below, where the swale seabirds smooth out,
Cathedral bells vein the tourist
Air with altar calls as
Choir boys in changing voices
Praise in changeless psalms.
                    I
                    Can hear the barnacles drying in the sun.
                    Waves spool small and lumpish like
                    Crystal snails and crystal feathers.
All is a matter of predilection,
                    Interrupted by lucidity.
                    I shall
Order the truth of history: preparing
The litter of earth, serving through
The replenishing complicity of
Glances exchanged with a lynx.
Nothing is voluntary.
                    Madness has cleared its throat here before.
                    Engines have expressed their tracks
                    Across our nostrils here before. An
                    Unknown body lies here beneath our grass,
Veining the brilliance and the agony of earth.
Around the cathedral the land bellies out,
Buckled by gravestones, forked walls, and halftimbered pubs.
                    As the mountains wear down,
                    I wear out, each rockslide
                    The fulfilling of my high desires.
                    And I
                    Must tourist go
But this beckoning farewell, unanimous in wings and stones,
                    Speechless in bones,
Strokes from the air

               A relentless annunciation,
Lifts into praise
A baptism by skulking breeze
               And of holy genitalia.

III. SWERVE SWAY SWOON

CURVED LINEARITY

        Almost a tree, the oleander bush
        Beside the fig tree bows beneath
        It, weighed down into a slumber
        During the day by heavy rain
Fiercely falling;
Its soaked branches blooming pink
Tentacles toward the window panes.
I need to get in there, beneath them
Both to pull at weeds snaking and
Stalking every different living thing.
I can do it but do not want to
Remember how, nor relive
        62 years gone.
Where is my inner voice
When I need it? I cannot hear
        It. Am I
Losing ear canal hair
From the white noise swirling
        There in its lair?
Or am I being too physical?
Is anything at all linear,
        Or are all things curved
        Secretly,
                Brilliantly?
Is it the curve, the lack of linearity,
        That shapes our mind to repeat
        Our blood, love, traces, flaws,
        And our bright brutality?
Doomed to similarity, the curved cell's awe
        Dies.

THE AROMA OF MOTHBALLS

All that bends against perturbations disappears.
My books, coins, pens, voices, or white noise rhyme
In my head, piled one atop another, bend and fade.
A beguiling, guileless infantry of light invades
        My brain. In my memory the aroma of mothballs,
        Body odor, hair spray, urine, and perfume comingle
        Every time I enter into the past into an old person's
        Uptown home: crossing the threshold with my father
        To paint window frames, replace sash cords, paint
        Baseboards, muck out an attic or an above ground
        Basement, or weed their gardens and mow their lawns.
Amorphous as fog, time bends, swirls, and curves.
If I knew how, I would throw away my selves to enter
The squalls of emptiness to know, not who, but what, I am.
        A working class son, I so disliked working
        For others. Wait for what, an ageless choking
        Surrounding
                Me insists?
                Always not quite ready to begin
        Something, to continue something, nor
                To complete something,
I have skipped the wars to yoke steady the wars within.

THE PENITENTIAL GIFT OF CONSCIOUSNESS

> The world is not a safe place for bodies,
> Except between breathing in and breathing out.

Our body wakes up in us, and we are awakened
To the penitential gift of consciousness. What don't
We know? There is nothing we do not know inside
Truer consciousness. Look! Wait! Don't judge!
The ego, self, spirit, and breath are one. Our body
Entire is a single meditation against forgetting
The mysterious charisma of not dying.

I've noted in my palm and stored below my wrist
Those dates and times I need to be out in the world.
Now, let's hope my lower back behaves.

In many places of the body we will sense, feel, and
Experience retold tales of mysteries, hopes, dreams,
Evil and good; of bold forgiveness, shame, devotion,
Beauty, and fear: The entire fabric of consciousness
And desire.

> Need we discover which beliefs block us
> From knowing and from understanding?
At the bend of winter over the band of exposed land
Always I am fascinated by how life smuggles into our
Hearts at an earlier age truths we at a later age accept,
And equally others we reject, without questioning.

With so much abundance of grace from
So many centuries of mayhem and grift,
We ought to be knowledgeable enough,
Evolved enough, to preview a future
Without blame, or punishment and shame.

THE CITY BELOW THE SEA

Neither the rose nor the thorn knows personal escape
As we do. Roses wither. Thorns sting or prick nonetheless,
Winter-hardening, darkening on dying, drying stems.

Above the river and the lake, the City below the sea
Holds secrets of which ropes and invisible threads
Yoke society and the individual as a twisting, threadbare
Culture intervenes.

Of which is a pathetic, wishful civilization still borne
Up, and rebreathed born whole? The essential human
Being is already a ghost among an air of ghosts.

Oh, my City, among others neither incompatible nor
Equivalent, bear me up to the joy and mercy of your
Questions: How old is this Universe? Do you own guns?
Do you believe in evolution? All lives matter, but
The persecuted matter more. When adversity reaches
Climax, joy in many is far off. In many others, near enough.

THE CALLING

When not influenced or pressed
By time or events, we are free
To notice that what is not yet
Now may be better than what is now.
Helplessness, inadequacy, denial
Of death or the afterlife, fear or
Hurt or anger will not become
Our calling.
      Blood migrates as clouds do, does
      Not seem to remain still as do clouds
      Like flour spilled across a blue counter.
Down here below the blue sky,
The same theme and variation,
As in all of art, science, and cosmologies
Of invisible orders of the Universe,
Permeate all brains of creatures surviving;
All stems and tubers and arteries of plants
And bodies arising. We will then no longer
Wordweasel and hesitate to sustain
      Communities living and blooming:
      Mineral, plant, animal, and human.
      For the longest moment though,
It is all politics and hatred of Gaia.
A deadend street, path, or alley
Is a beginning, because we must
Turn around, turn back even,
Drenched with the sweetsour sweat
Of a new anticipation that may even
Lead to nowhere, depending on
Whether we hesitate or run, hitting
      The ground before memory's fog
      Swarms in, seeking ghosts.
      Horse or hearse, vehicle or obstacle
Basket or casket, the armored carriage's
Glistening heart darkens at a heart's ending.
Now, as each generation learns, the reach
Of a planet's hidden personal worlds tarnish
The embrace of missions of peace. The appeals

To the worm of war are a long distance agony
For help, as nations stretch, twist, and grunt,
        Encompassing their scaly, predaceous centipede
        Arms across Gaia's soulsour nerves.

EVE'S BOOK

Eve in the sacred wild must have tempted Adam
With a Book, not an apple; nor sex and honey,
Nor the conscious light from her yet ungated,
Unvisited vagina, which is why mostly men
Believe they must study and read hastily to taste
The throat-soothing nectar of eye-opening orgasmic
Truth.

Some things go and come back: New things leap
in: Lost carpet patterns on the blessing floor,
Ongoing adventures awakening, while we sleep
Leaning at the threshold against an open door.

Between Eve's fingers into the oil eggs of birth
And death drop. She is awake now.

Ideologies, a revenge of opposites, abide.
Her mind shifts to no intent in particular
As hunger drifts off astride shy laughter
In the shirt cuff against her face.
Her gaze unravels Life.

With eyes raised to the sunlight sprinkling
Through a blushing rain, she reaches out
Through bashful trees for myriad seeds
Sprouting before her unfenced beneficence.

CIMARRON'S COMPLINE

I doubt
at this canonical hour
it's possible
to paraphrase a poem,
to count on the protection
of fiction.

So how can I depict these lives?
How
might
I?
How will I draw in the landscapes
that span the escape of their blood,
of these ancient gods straitjacketed
within us,
into feuds and moods
eternal,
universal,
original?

We are the problem:
outflows with opposing ends.
Within us
contradiction can be
positive and productive,
like the synagogue in the mosque
that we see in the architecture's
devout allusions
to nineteenth century Upper West Side
German Jews;
or in the church temples of Asia Minor
Orthodox Christians.
Or like the unmindful allusions to the Buddha's
revelation of the certainty of Oneness that
we see in the Ottoman's devout finality to
abolish the mystery of nations and religions,
as we also observe in the gravedigger
relentlessness of Marx and Engels.

Where in the four corners of our education
Are the revelations of our multiple experiences?

Unconscious congruity
is the wealth
of
our unshakeable,
incongruent faiths.
Gardens.
Landscapes.
Visions.
Temples.
Halls.
Dungeons.
Trizoid. Trizophrenic.
Trabzon.

In the French Quarter
the frontal lobe lust
of forthright tourists
illumines
the night of the Southshore.
Among
them often
I
stroll, pause, glide, strut, slide, and slip on.
Slip on.
Slip away.
All of this history of
Islamic Europe
and the
Christian East
is not as simple as we
        would like to make of it,
Mahdi,
        my friend. We will one day reveal.
We are the problem: human
families with opposing ends,
darker, more demonic,
and more predictable

in our desires
and more unpredictable
in our
will,
deeds,
and destiny.
Recognizable
but afraid of recognition,
as any brain that does not
perceive its own ruminations,
I
sit here at the edge of the universe
this evening
on one side of the veil, and also here
at a Café du Monde table on the opposite
side;
a

partitioned

soul,
among friends, amidst city visitors,
hungering for recall,
catatonic amidst
omniscience
omnipresence
and forgetfulness.
Justice hasn't yet drafted omnipresent
government informers to rubberneck at our elbows
to eyeball the secrets that we may be cupping
to our laps
or to eavesdrop in on the weedy words clamped
behind our lips.
But always striving to spot arresting connections,
I look over my shoulders constantly of late
whenever my comrades bemoan over cups of café au lait
the lack of heroes and the bombardment of censorship
among the pages, screens, and waves of our media;
also of Russia, Turkey, Iran, Saudi Arabia, North Korea.
"How brave acts of conscience
are inversely proportional
to how much freedom citizens
enjoy," Julian suggested.

"Marching against the government
in Washington would not be as
courageous as assembling against the
royals in Makkah," agreed Mahdi.
"No wonder the Republicans and the Royals
adopt and defend one another," I tossed out.
Each lifted eyebrows in acknowledgement.

"But, Cimarron, our freedoms are meant to encourage
us to engage in Democracy,"Thessaly scowled. "And in
a democracy this takes very little risk," I connected.
We connected. She smiled.
I smiled behind a sip of coffee.
The night light from the street lamps
                sparkled in her green eyes
                and diamoned blue her purple black
                        skin.
The early October air sparkled with the fine mist
of evening rain beneath the street lamps. Earlier,
in the late afternoon just before dusk, shafts of sunlight
crystaled the slight rain as the sun descended into the
East Bank below the shadows of the Vieux Carré.
                I sensed the historical worry of slaves long gone
                armoring my breast. A doctor might say it was
                a tightening in my chest.
"But why would these things worry us if we are not really
doing anything wrong?" Phantom insisted, stabbing the table.
                I worry even as I write these memories.
                Is this my act of conscience a criminal act now?
                Will this my act of conscience interfere
                        with my relationships?
Our president then either did not understand
                democracy or rejected it outright.
                He scolded us that the will
                of protesters against the new
                        world order he was reconstructing
                        in a freed Iraq does not count,
                        that the opinions of mere citizens
                                are irrelevant.
Sumer is a place of death now.

His shadow still presumes over a democracy
        where his authority arises
        from the will of a sovereign
        people who do not know this.
His decisions are yet beyond our control.
We can only respond to their consequences:
A man with no plan.
        Participatory Sumer is a place of death now.
Perhaps Heaven has sent him to us
so that our poems may possess more
meaning, that at last a self-indulgent America
        may discover the parabolic verb.
I love my country enough to risk
awakening each morning in its wrath.
A sudden storm parsed the city
        on impetuous
            airs.
Thessaly had floated here up the sidewalk
toward our table in yellow sandals,
her knees, draped softly behind flowing
        linen white,
        nudging
        the night.

CASCADE

An obscene sun flooding the bandstand
Is an unusual moment at an outdoor concert
Performing above a bend in the river at the end
Of a street in a still small country town in August.
Southshore born, Northshore prospered, gray
Heads in baggy khakis and skintight skirts nod
And bob attuned to the rhythms of high school
And the odors of darkened, unparented front rooms.

The day drops, a scrim in the late afternoon
Breeze as the world rotates and the sun moves.
I am on the verge of avoiding that I no longer
Know how to admit my flaws, and realize that it
Is my nation's flaws avoiding admission, not mine,
For my nation is me and I am my nation.

My nation has lost the grace and courage to kill
And not murder, to vanquish and not maim.
Like our youth, we are but yet a young country
Reveling in drive-by and fly-over immolations of
The skin and spirit of dignity.

At a time when fourteen million grim Americans are out
Of work, how can I be content with time for the river
Below, a splendid descending dusk, and bracing music all
Around us here at the edge of town as the nation plunges
Into war again, here in a nation where nation building has
Died for us, and not by us for others across the planet?

A world of one's own may be fluent and unsteady.

This split between I and me is an awakened colonial tenet
In my groin as my nation creates me as its spectral double.
Colonizer and colonized, we now both hold the mirror
Before us, unfamiliar and unrecognizable, side by side
Temple against temple, shoulder to shoulder, nerve to nerve,
As I trip and stumble on the Northshore into the depth and arc
Of my soul's Cavalry Calvary toward the Men's lavatory.

PEACE AND WAR

I want to be   We need you
sent from war.   where language and situation
                                      become us.
Home   .   .   Freedom
beckons my senses   chronicles your senses
soothes my sleep   .   .   disciplines your weapons
receives my wakening.   honors our frightened allies.

Peace is a flock of meadow birds   Peace is an outerspace hospital
feeding on blood oranges from my mouth.   of newborns nursed after dying.

War is scarecrow carrion   War is unearthed architecture
becoming sloven tongues.   glimpsing privileged government

AN ABRUPT MORTALITY

I caught myself this morning noticing life lies
As personal myths of the self ignoring infinite
Consciousness that is not the body beyond words
But is source where I am space. The heel-dragging
Narrative dogging our heels is the death of ego

As we know it, like leaving a novel that we are
In the middle of on an empty bus seat next to us,
Or on a plane stuffed in the back pocket of the seat
In front; or our fiddle on the metro in the rack
Above our consciousness. These days I remember
Forgotten nostalgia.

How is it possible to know something
Others do not know, unless I am born
Knowing? And then there are those thrown
With the knowledge of knowing, kilned
By a self larger than self.

Yesterday has come and gone. Today passes;
Tomorrow, a feeling, while beyondmorrow
Is unimaginable. How many days are there
After the morrow, actually? Step forth
Into the light. Whisper your response to me

To the door and back. The jowls of the fog
Over the river are sagging. When will the faces
Come forward? When will they seek closure?
Give me the goblet in the center to drink constant,
Beautiful, sincere problems from.

ANNE'S COMING IN, HER GOING OUT

We keep each other's secrets, stumbling
Into wars behind blinkered eyes with
No hint of how to halt. Whistling, Death's
Arrow dipped into Anne's waters, sucking
The capillaries to desert. Let's imagine her
Death without a fear of death; nor with
Envy or jealousy. The vibrations in words
Is all that matters, embossed along
A gatefold of heroic moments.

Hers for us has been the kind of death
We inward feared would shear asunder
Our clear headedness at any moment. Her
Radiant skin and fearless confidence, despite
For years annoying death as it hunts
The natural world, shoved back against
Dying almost any day or night. Yet
Death is a democratic promise.

When cancer sneaked up behind her liver,
We had an offertory of neither words nor
Looks falling false like holy water or incense
Arising. Our simple staring could not lie.
Moral negligence often misses glancing details.
Because before death we are bowed-down
And bow-tied, the outcome of hints is nothing
More than a farewell to hints; as the body gripping
Ambition bids so long to this desire this time,
And to griping

THESSALY AT TWILIGHT

   Space is hardly ever innocent.
It forces us to consider time as dark and light,
Dim and bright. By 5:00, morning and evening,
The sky falls through tall, bareback trees. Dead,
Cracked, winddriven limbs scuttle on crinkled knees,
Winter nearing carefully across dampdusty grass.
Black maids pick peppergrass early in Taylor Park.
Live oaks tent Louisiana forever. Thunderbolts day
Or night again, again and again, ionize the New Orleans
Twilight in arterial white against blue or black sky
Up Napoleon Avenue from the River to Carrollton
And Lark.
   Thessaly halfway out the back door
Forgot her glasses on the fireplace mantle.
A sandal slips from her foot as she twirls
Back after them. Outside again, bending
Over for the sandal facing her upside
Down, she bounds across the back porch
Onto bricks below splintering steps;
One sandal afoot, the other in hand.
The cool air simmers.
   Slipping the other sandal on as she sat
On a low step, shoulders hunching against the new,
Hand railing, she senses the moment to be a friend
And wants every next friend, enemy, and moment
To be a moment like this moment in perpendicular
Time.

Her body's branching shadow, barren of anyone's
Touch, darkening now through the assembling
Twilight by dusk, desires only moments, not
Events or practices, or activities. Free: no longer
Anyone's daughter, no America to take up her part,
Nor yet anyone's companion. She has no one: no
Ọlọ́run or Philip or Cyril or Alex or Orestes to tell
Her what to believe, or how to begin the journey
Of life of her ancient youthful heart.

Make tomorrow come.

A FLUTE ROACH

An idle amateur musician, he simply puts his flute aside
atop the nearest piece of furniture or shelf or mantel,
wherever he happens to be in his apartment
when he ceases practicing, to pee, to smoke, to make
a cup of tea or coffee; or to swig more gin. This mostly at
night, except for weekends, because during the day, during
the work week, he drives a city bus.

At night, once he's gone off to sleep, the flute will be
abandoned, left lingering anywhere. But no
matter where it's planted, especially if it's on the floor
next to his easy chair, there is this one massive roach that always
finds it. Well, massive for a roach: fat thumb size in length and width.
A mutant thing, most likely; it locates the flute by its fragrant emanations:
traces of the bus driver's breath no doubt, of gin or a sandwich or
buttered spaghetti or toothpaste.
No woman's mouth has left its smear on this man's lips for ages;
so it's not the expected taste of the lingers of lust that will nightly draw
the roach toward the flute, but only the imperceptible ambient traces
of sweetly stale human breath swirling in and out of the finger
holes of the French flute like invisible fumes that are part
of the forces of nature of this creature's existence
expectations, and experiences.
Each night, at the cockroach's first hint of these human scents,
evading a tiny bulb of light from the hallway wall, it crouches near and nearer
and then right up to the shining familiar but unknown thing that we
know to be a flute. Because the cockroach's brain is spread
throughout its body, its exoskeleton stiffens with
anticipation. As it spies its own reflection
once again in the metallic mirror, its
spiracles breathe hard and deep, and,
in mounting excitement, it skitters
back and forth along the length
of the flute,
chasing its narcissistic
double. It caresses the flute
with its antennae, explores it
with its short front crawlers.

It will be decades yet, at least, before
periambientsonic physics figures out mathematically how
it is that sound, though it fades from human hearing, never ceases,
never dies, but bounces, floats, and flows on endlessly around us,
filling out the open air, where all sounds make way for one another.
In fact, this fact is something that insects have a sense of and would
know that they had a vibrational sense of it if they, in fact,
knew that they know anything at all of tones and colors.
For a while, the cockroach flits in and out of one finger
hole after another,
sensing fading, receding vibrations as it playfully
flutes in and out of the bus driver's instrument.

It scuttles, jigs, and jags back
and forth through traces of circles
within circles of past-played notes. Eventually,
apparently exhausted or satiated, it calms down.

As its spiracles breathe in more of the human fumes
emitting from the flute, its heart rate slows down,
and it becomes perfectly, exquisitely stilled.
It remains that way all night, relentless, reverential
before the flute, until the first hint of dawn
breaks through
the mostly lightless hush
and lush of night.

PENELOPE'S DAUGHTERS

In childhood we were told by mothers and nuns
Not to tell stories, not to lie; so a lie is a story.
Telling stories is sinful.

A moment of space participating in divine
Distance, we shift our way through harassed
Efficiency on our way out, nudged toward
Eternal knowledge. Early morning gunfire
Leaves three dead in every city. Fewer
Women now sit oceanside dutifully among
The rocks and driftwood while their men
And sons surf blocks of ocean and sea.
Nowadays straddled and balanced along
The horizon of their board, they also find
Their sway's swerve in the waves' barrel
To pebble, bay, and sand, refusing to crawl
Like crabs to shore, especially at the end
Of the dry day. Roaring back to town,
Outdistancing the slow, bright clouds,
"You should have been there!" they shout
                    To the sky.

          In the sportsman's paradise these days, fewer women
               Leer in mirrored distances, pacing empty spaces
Around the home while their men squat hidden in camouflage
To kill deer, ducks, or wild hogs. From mid November to mid
January entire families now bunker down in the rented wild,
Fondling in wait their marksmen instruments like banjos or
Accordions, in wait to stalk and steal life from life. Clay
Robbing clay, as resurrected Lazarus, on Cyprus, once laughed.
               At every trigger pull,
               They reload the Civil War.
          In traditionalist societies, the woman is the one
          Whose heart knows who the father of this son
          Or that other daughter is. The father, an unreliable
          Variable, like the unreliable narrator in modern
          Fiction. The mother's knowledge is a liable constant,
          Though the man may be the village's libelous griot,
          Or among the majority of storytellers in the world.

HYPATIA, BOOKLADEN, FORLORN

They ride me bareback, then move me aside, out.
Theocratic men. I move. Move on, led as a raped
          Passenger in carriages defiled:
Penniless, stripped of the infrared hum of my
Body's particle waves momentum. We are but
Riders and passengers booked in a good book.
They do not understand the drift carrying them
Through the centuries. A good book unexpected
Found is never a completion nor even a conscious
Continuity, but an unconscious, elated continuation
                    Of the life
                    Of the mind. Riding, ridden, bareback.
          I've never wanted these syllables and sentences
          To become autobiographical but to reach out
          Toward galaxies in the brain yet unknown as
          A mosaic in the brain; as the boundaries of blood
          And borders, though we separated off 80 million
          Years ago, mapped by forests and meadows, country
          And city. Never a binary curve, a sweep of meadowlarks
          Thrust suddenly into a split-second swoop leftward
          Southeast over the Lake to the tune of a Honky Tonk
          Roma's steel guitar, twisting into a sweep eastward
                    Downriver into the Delta.
Scientific myths, mythical sciences, though
When they do not convince also instruct.
In freefall freewill, our sacred spirits, open
To mystery that never stills, saturating
The atmosphere unseen and unfelt,
Are not hands dealing blind. If home is the last
          Stop, the journey is home to find.

IZMIR IN LATE WINTER

I have always loved the ones who desire to cry
I have always loved the ones who desire to laugh

Winter winds will be departing soon.
Snow surrounding the city, crisscrossing
The slopes of the ghettoized hills,
Is beginning to melt. Sliding, twirling,
Twisting, drifting downward unsensed
Along sporadic nightly rains descending
During the dark, new angels and demons
Take root, squatting bluntly, thickly down
Into the cold, muddy, watermaddened earth.
Scent, a solid in nature like color, can fall
On the face just as streetlight can, and linger.
In the parks, the imprisoned stench of dried
Dog and cat urchin pee and poop released by the rains
From among the soaked soil and soaking blades
Assault our recovering orientalist faces lowered against the wind
Under hat brims, umbrellas, or steepled hands.
It is impossible to turn our face upward to the
Stars and moons that are not there.
          Why are we even out on a night like this one,
Except to enter an idle café or an unexpected
Play, without a season ticket, at a half-empty
House? I have always loved the decisive city
Desiring to cry and to laugh, that chooses
Neither one against the other, but strips naked
Even in an indecisive winter, awaiting the spring rains.
As in my snowless city, New Orleans, sloped
Along the inner brim of a bowl, Izmir's bay, docks,
Ports, and piers also perch the rim of a crescent,
Where ships navigate history, memory, disbelief.

          These two Crescents each all year long attract
Tourists and visitors: one for its exotic otherness, its
History; the other for the indifferent difference of
The enclosed Insouciance of its Vieux Carré, whose
Residents, denizens, and outoftown frat boys add to

Or pay no attention at all to the stench of dog urine
And feces up alleyways, or along gutters.

      Perhaps it's time for unbelief, to be done with
Heaven and the dogmas of war, of the gods,
Rabbis, priests, and imams embattled. There are
Some nights when a city's lit, shrewd eyes catch
Me in an outrighteous frankness, as if it recognized
Me, had seen me here before, as if I were a warrior
On leave from a ship or the trenches, or escaped
From a rest asylum, daydreaming nestled in the
Evening heart of the city, wishing I had a better
Appointment in life. All I can wish for it, however,
Is that if it can read my mind, it will find for itself
There exultation, admiration, grace, and purpose.

IV. AT A LOSS FOR WORDS

ANATOLIA

　　　　　Like castoff faded toy blocks palmed from a junk
Yard pile, not an antique shop shelf, the drab
Overnight squats terraced up and down along
The perches, crevices, ledges, and trenches in the
Hills surrounding Bursa, Izmir, Ankara—all
The byways, highways, and freeways toward Antep—
Are a sight for sore eyes for those who dwell there,
Squatting, perching; and a sore sight for bright eyes
For those born and nurtured down below, in the valley
Or across sea cities and suburbs, toward Thessaloniki
Beyond the poor, the blight.
　　　　　The Mississippi and the Aegean ready their waters
For battle. Before war, civil or international, finally comes,
The first skirmishes are truncated, endless prattle. Then
The dignified, indignant surge of thumping, whistling
Hissing, whooshing, lashing, and flailing of battle fire
Intended to end war by snuffing out a life, one life,
Any life, definitively. But those who survive do dig trenches
Through shadows with the limbs of the dead again. We'll
Take it down below now. Waiting above only makes it harder
　　　　　　　To bare the missiles.

GARTER AND THIMBLE

Though it neither maims nor heals,
The Flag, there in nodding glory,
          An unshredded icon in the heart
          Casting light over a Constitution
When the Constitution, penned by Beauty
Or misread by Ghoulishness, speaks alone in loneliness,
          Will utter forever also on end. We might
          Never have sown this creature of cloth
                    Into existence
                    In ceaseless memory.
          For only a Constitution chants the truth
          Of any brave or any dark part of the heart.

          Mothers   Nor do they resist
          Never desire war   An exiled date of birth.
          In neighborhoods   They keep the order
          Of hooded secrets.   Of the thimble intact.
                    The order of the garter
                    Rides the lioness' back.
We desire no more than what pleases the homeless
Mother taken in. Only she can part the reddest of seas.
Because Adam exceeded the limits of natural pleasure,
Leaning into the fruit of desire for a second bite,
                    The Reed Seas
No longer lie spread open before us, beckoning us
To make way for helpful heresies from the Bosporus
To the Tiber toward one enlightenment after another.
Both flag and constitution bend under the gales
                    Of civil war.
Marriage should never be a backup plan.

WITHOUT LIGHT

"You are so thin," he sneered. "You must fast
Obviously often, to expiate your sins no doubt."
The Question is clear: What is the origin, nature,
Evolution, and destiny of matter; of matter's time
And space; of wisdom, of wisdom's integrity, rigor,
Goodness, simplicity, nobility, and knowledge? Fate
Is in our hands. The Question creates our brain.

To experience the gaze behind what we see, whom
We look to, we must experience interior equations
Glancing back, verifying the real and the appearing.
May we possess reality without science and religion?
Or do they possess us?

My eye possesses the dust of night and a full moon,
The splatter of daylight and the blinding rain, and the
Voices whispering in my brain attuned to the infinitesimal
Separation of each thin stem of leaves knuckled along
Bare, nude, naked limbs of trees imploring continuity.
What happens outside or beyond us happens also within.
                    Deeper.
The stars of our mortality evaporate into intense depths,
Heat brittling apart, bristling into elementary particles
Of quantum life, each life ending in a blinding implosion.
Time and space subside, suspend, meaningless. Collapsing
Within quantum gravity, where we each dust off, until we flow
Low again, may I next time be reborn under
                    Different laws?
                    Without light,
                    Immortality is in the dark.

BLOODY BORDERS

1

Stripped naked, the next households
were ordered to the rim of their grave.
Numbed into duty, they waited their turn to step down into
the pit brimming with the dead before them. The father,
placing a hand on his daughter's head, with his other hand turned
her chin up toward his breaking face. His mother softly stroked temple hymns from her
throat into his infant's ear. Armed guards barked at the family after them to peel

away their rags. Two families
shuffled and squirmed at their
mound of earth and naked stumbled and slipped
into the ditch scarred out for them from the land.
The soldiers' guns silenced the hymn and stilled the tremors quaking
in their limbs. Sitting along the edge of the open tomb, they teased ammunition from
their stroked weapons, shattering bone, shearing muscle and brain, of the no longer
stoked living. What has changed then, since 1941?

2

On this evening now, across the gulf,
the jagged light of the neighboring mountains of Jordan
shifted through oranges, reds, purples, and lastly into blues,
as the sun crimsoned the clouds above the blue mountains before disappearing.
In descending darkness, a full moon grayed mountain summits, as the lights of
Eilat and Aqaba sparkled the night. The Red Sea reflect back the neon of tourist

scows on this Shabbat. It's Eid
al-Adha in Israel. Darboukas
and the Qur'an rhymed the night air. Over campfires
along the beach, Palestinians tended to coffee and
barbecues. Jewish youths farther up crooned American rock lyrics
in English and Hebrew to a strummed guitar and boombox. Why am I ambivalent?
Mostly empty near the Egyptian border, amidst the sunset of the southern beach,

an earlier flock of seagulls swooped
and soared above gently shimmering waves
lapping above a mosaic of pebbles and shells. The wildflower
sanctuary and coral reefs of the Negev had lulled us into
a moment's forgetfulness among endangered families of gazelles, eagles,

and falcons. In my sad bones and sore eyes I remembered conversations of the beauty
of the legendary, sacred land of the Marsh Arabs along the border of Iran and Iraq.

3

Where is Eden now? The lush
tributaries of the Euphrates
are soaked dry in executions, chemicals, and bombs.
A high court in Belgium indicts the bloodsoaked chronicles
and sadistic flowering roses of Saddam and Sharon as our nation
rattles dice in the dynastic back rooms of dismissive sighs. Blueblood presidents, like
elite generals, always gamble their war of choice. The people are never their mission,

unless they belong to someone else.
Interest and belief caress the guns.
Our nation, once a revolution in its youth, now carves
out revolt and rebellion in the world's neighborhoods.
Loudmouth demagogues splatter blindly against our nightly screens.
Politicians shield their confusing heart in battles of bombast. Fathers once pushed for
the diplomat's peace. Now sons sweep the world with an adviser's broom of war.

4

Our balance of power is an unbalanced Eden.
Our nation reports that we have no funds for
health and education as it negotiates aid with new Europe.
We are made poor and poorer as the military becomes rich
and wealthier in protective gear and weaponry. Our paradise needs no
protecting angel at the gate. All men are now avengers. Peace like war has never come
cheap, though the costs are not the same. Ambivalent are our blood, heart, and brain.

All dissent looms seditious to the youth
who squanders his action affirmatively;
who rebels amidst his privileged wealth along the cheerleaders'
halls of unearned learning, while the people struggle for rights
more civil than the envious rivalries of slothful, covetous, guffawing boys; who
soon becomes thoughtfully tightlipped, reflecting himself in men as dull as tonguetied
bells, as the lights of libraries across our cities extinguish the joys

of books and come on again in suburban
citadels. As for the supercilious strutting
before lecture halls, the humanists dismiss objectivity
as inherently oppressive, while the scientists disparage
qualitative interpretation as mere personal opinion. We create on earth

sheer absences as we reduce and force one another into enmity. Compassion
has died. Once the very incarnation of liberation and human rights, we now
court suicide.

What has changed then, since 1941

except for my birth

as we stroke, caress, the smartest gun?

HEARTS APART

The hesitant "And …."
Teetering at the edge of her palm slipped away,
As her hand came to rest convinced at her heart.

She had no more
Arguments in her breast, nor in any part of the room,
The house, the garden, the aches and acres of lawn

On the back road
Of the small town where they came to settle down.

His destiny, built upon a life of deeds, his will and unseen
Desires, in a declining body not yet breaking apart then,
Except for a vague soreness in his wrists, knees,
Ankles, and heart,

He hesitated often to step on cracks, spill salt, walk under
Ladders; to demure before black cats prowling about
Among trillions of microbial flits fulfilling the air.
Everywhere we breathe in, she knew, we, expanding like
Our own universe, also breathe out epidermal settlements
Of dust among mites as indifferent as we are blind to truth.
Why should she be happy only after he passes away, she
Thought constantly? Then one dawn, she had imagined
His morning wheezing for birds in the attic
Or behind the eaves.

One, perhaps even each of them, might once have
Silently recalled as if at prayer when
She his Grand Canyon,
He her Mount Everest,
Unaware of bone and hinge,
They paused, hovered, skimmed
At will their fingers across
Skin addressing each other's
Unknown skeletons.

Those of us who come visiting now, to pay respects, linger.

THE PULL

Differences nor similarities alone will attract
Us to one another. Nor will similarities draw us
In, toward, without understanding, differences.
Without similarities, our differences will not
Evolve unique persons. Not defined by time,
We must make our problems our solutions
And disregard the rumblings of rumors.

Until death do we part, they say. True enough.
True also is that until another's death do we
Gravitate at funerals toward each other;
A reunion of sorts, I suppose, among
Condolences leaning, pressing, into
One another's shoulder.

Those people are not serious, those among our
Leaders elected to follow the will of reason
And common wit. They sell out the yet unborn,
Beings whom they do not know, cannot fathom,
With a dreary tyranny. Now even the outskirt
Venues of my mind end in cul-de-sacs because I
Cannot figure a thing out any more. I no longer
Grasp why politicians lie against one another,
Fabricate sheer nonsense. I would love to ignore
History, to not realize opponents in government
Have always done so, that nothing at all is new.

Aspiring kindness and mystery simultaneously, why
Did the vessels break at the moment of creation, spill
Forward, slipping downward from the hand of the gods
Of time? We are in an age of dismantled selves,
This twenty-first century. Our hands turn
Into aimless keyboards, our fingertips into
Unalphabetical order.

Everything is forever, isn't it? The eternal,
Perpetual of This and That always takes forever.
Along the northern rim of the Caribbean where I

Was born, where I live again, crime once more
Stalks our streets years hence since provocative
Katrina peeled off her veils as she danced naked
Above our heads, as federal waters breached our levees,
Chrismating our feet, knees, and throat with brackish
Benediction.

THE STRUGGLE ODE

I have often wondered why
it is neighbors who are not
also friends. Across our garden
and yard:

I

sense that my neighbor

loves his wife,
believes in discipline, rule, and denial, as he tucks
his army blanket across the boozy stupor of her chest,
and leaves her to the gathering evening chill prattling
across the patio.

Normally, Rwanda's rivers swell
with red clay when the rains
come. This year the shallows also swell with
        desecrated black bodies bleached
                purple white
        by the rich eroding red earth:
first, old men, soldiers, boys, girls, women; then the live
babies drowning downstream. Upon Africa's escaping
faces reign mute hunger and holloweyed confusion.

When the struggles
are ancient, there
is no distinction between soldier
and civilian in the human hunt.

Fighting only to stay alive means fighting
only to escape from the repetitive future.
Heads of state have never been outraged
Enough to say that we are
                sisters
                and
                brothers.

IN DARKNESS AN UNFINISHED FORCE

She had no intention of looking up
away from her hands but the dark
opulence without struck her eye
as she sat at her desk
inside an unfinished bookish feeling
beside the garden window.

Nor has she ever had an intention
of rummaging around within
as scenes from years ago
of her lack of humility or compassion
at specific moments worried in
her heart's desire to be only ordinary.

The alert shock of self-revelation
was immense, as if the graying wind
outside had broken through the pane
and sucked the simmering aromas
from the kitchen, for she never thinks
of herself as unkind.

We are all victims of war.
I wonder often if we realize
how hapless crime and war
daily hardly make us sober.
The only compensation is
that history is never over.

So what can she do now in order
not to be just a portrait silhouette
in the shadows of the day brought
into her room by an approaching storm
as the gift of hard, heavy rain outside
the gift of guilt and remorse inside?

At peace with herself over years of
repressed denial, locked away
against conscious loopholes,

sticking points, or problems,
at sad moments her one desire,
which she also harbors now,
has always been, when she passes
on from this life, to be neither
female nor male, but only
a presence, if she could ever word
it precisely, of elemental essence
floating off and away, up and out.

There is no moon out for her
as day falls into night and she
never seems to wonder why
as if the question would never
ever exist to die upon her lips.
It's left to you and me to wonder
about the hidden bright-eyed
sun of indifference, the shadowed
moon of unconsciousness,
the lack of fear, to which
she has been loyal.

BEERS AND TRANSFORMATIONS

When the Earth was mud and void, naked
And wild, unformed and unreplenished,
Sephten Jealous Sit departed his small town,
Warm breath dried on paranoid
Lips, to die on diseased ground.

History, silent, alone
As maps, will not deny his name.

He was taught to hide
The essence of what he is
To give no warning, nor ease;

A pillow over his face,
A heart of barbiturates.

      Man born of woman
Always seems a clear lament
To Sephten Sit, ramrod, unbent.
A life concerns change.

What he couldn't chew, he drank.
Like all drunks, he loved all life.
Cyrille upon his flesh.
This grind upon the table.
This grin upon ancient tablets.
The Gods upon their souls.
Brutality, gentleness,
Beers and transformations, blend.
      Women to men like Sit
Are interchangeable, voiceless,
Homogeneous;
An anonymous body
An essential distraction.

Cyrille? Cyrille, part this, part that,
Kurdish, Turk, Greek, African Jew:
Grandmothers upon grandmothers

Upon grandmothers: in this,
He desired her for her mosaic passion. Often,
Seeking a thing European, an imagined thing,
To no good end, he would caress from her face
Centuries of aches until pain came bursting forth
As a loved, perceived dusk through her glistening,
Ineluctable skin.

IN SEASON

Black or White, gay or straight, young or old,
The Southern Male is a Thing to behold,

Spick and span in his camouflage jacket and cap
In and out of deer and duck season's carefree lap.

In season, he pins one knee at the neck of a slain doe;
One fist clenches steady a flag, a rifle, or a bow.

The other palm lifts the dead head, its alert thumb
And fingers splaying the eyes open to avert the dumb

Dead stare toward the camera. Sometimes the new
Or young spouse poses on the new kill. The beast's

Freed spirit senses its host's end had come and casts
Over the lifeless body's snarled face the sweet, fervent

Ecstatic piety of an Ancient Asia Minor Saint's glance
Skyward.

IRISH BAYOU

My head rolled
absently toward the
window along the back
of my easy chair; just as
I, slipping off, gazed out,
imagining the dark bush
burning green outside,
beckoning me as it dipped
and spread its branches
beneath the gentle wind
passing on eastward
aflame across my yard.
I nodded off to sleep.

I did not want to take a nap
midday today, this Purim,
Pascha, Nawruz weekend.
But I dreamed of Irish Bayou,
its sheet of water placid,
like blood coagulated in steel.
From eyelid to rapid eyelid
the bumblebees humming
there among the magnolias
and azaleas buzzed about
my brain.

Behind my agitated, fluttering,
closed eyes, scenes flickered
through my mind of limbless
uniforms drowning under tanks
and planes wherever Nero
or Caligula might have, like our
current occupant, tapped dance,
across the Tigris and Euphrates
cresting in blood beneath his soles
polished with the spit of White House
bootblacks.

In the background tuned down
just ever so slightly above hearing
on the radio is news no different
from last week's of deaths enormous
in number, senseless in enormity.
Accounts of mayhem obedient
unto death bombard the planet
rotating in my brain and universe.
Prayer, moaning, groaning, mumbling,
shrugging, mewling arise like smoke
and incense around the soul's gnarled hands.
Crocuses and caucuses bloom in the land
this election year. In a month or two
the sad, sleepless heat will descend across
the lake, the bayous, the swamps, the river;
and I will be awake as always in a nation that
has attempted over the past eleven years or more
to render so much of the world obsolete,
and I will be joyful on a landscape of weary
liberty for just being alive in a time of
idiocy.

THE LITTLEST THINGS

The littlest things
scurry across barbwire,
electrical lines,

my nerves afire about
the littlest of things

so consequential.
From the physics of the sky
foul things storm-footed alight:

humming, slugs, remorse, tasteless
fear, governmental madness

gently encamping
internal security,
curfews, tribunals
with butterfly bombs soaring
from the baying vaginas
of State phalluses
disguised as safeguarding crafts.

Diseases, landmines,
natural disasters, and wars:
the mastery of statecraft,
elude us all times.

We are studious as field horses,
grazing as we step, nibbling,
never gazing up at all, nose
in the grass of inattention,
until quiet discomforted
discomforts us.

PRESERVERS SURVIVE

If America dissolves zigzag in the air
Or upsy-daisy in the oceans and seas,
Doubts, floating motives, and schemes,
And dreams of our fathers, dreams from
Our mothers, will survive as collections in
Pritzker, Delgado, McKenna, and Frick
Survivors' Museums.

Like the late evening shiver of flowers
Overcome by the hug of darkness,
Whatever we may think of Cyrus The Lesser
In the shared daylight of hindsight,
We know that amoral Haman The Puppet will
Make us rise up to heal the curvature
Of our moral spine to push back against
All that he with neither brain nor heart
Represents as we shoulder sadness,
Alienation, grief, trauma, outrage.

How might we learn to enfold inside
Out to experience other dimensions
Otherwise sensed but unseen when
We walk a talk in shoes not the right size?

Dumb luck like sacred evolution is just
Nuts, and parasites never die. Whatever
Belief tent hovers above us, the bubble
We inhabit within blocks the real world
Out. No one's illusion unveils reality's
Lout to free us.

JULIAN CONTEMPLATES HIS THUMBNAIL

No doubt the waning or waxing
Crescent of the moon
Has been likened to a thumbnail
By some Ottoman court poet. But who
Has given thought to the thumbnail
Beyond this likeness?

Who among us has noticed
That the crescent resembles,
Or in truth may be, the nail
Or scale of the Divine Digit?
Or is this a sliver of Divine Light
Emanating from the Divine Eyeball
As the Divine Eyelid initially
Opens upon us all in perpetuity,
As the Whole Eye itself phases
Across eternity?

I used to dislike posing answerless
Questions, until I got it that
The best questions have no answers,
Only responses, and are therefore
Holy and are a form of worship.

When I gaze past the slats of blinds
Through the window pane out across
At pine trees, the mulberry and fig trees,
The lotus lilies upon the mirroring pond,
I know that this growth is not worshipping me,
But is venerating upward as do we.

V. MONUMENTS AND RUINS

WINDOW

I sit at that window often
wherever my window might be
in a classroom
in my apartment
in my office
in a coffeehouse by the sea;
in anyone's home
hosted
by ritual
by routine
by unspoken polite misunderstanding.

All windows are mine,
portals where all things
might be expanding:
proximate space
proximate time
proximate distance
even more proximate proximity.

Proximate minds
proximate bodies
space and time
rippling free
beyond frameless
windows
borders
periphery;
frontier
birth
cradle;
candle glows;
deaths
burials
coffins
caskets
pyres
outflows.

A window and its wall
are an unskilled crew
of acolytes ministering
to my meditations.

The wall that wraps a window
torments my view, my flights
Of fancy spiriting through.

Wifeless for two years
at three six month intervals
I begin to wonder what
husbandry means
on fallow ground;
dry husband bound
by no one to comfort
to coax
to console
to cajole
to hug
to humbug
to stare at
to glare at
to gaze upon.

The wall is my companion.

For almost two years
I will not see her skin age,
at six month intervals,
as it has.

My home is on another planet
and so am I.

In my sleep these days,
in a single peignoir
of sheen she is malt liquor
the temper of Greek tsipouro
or the gold of Turkish tea.

What am I doing here,
teaching others ideas that flit
from one window through another?
What boils have I lanced, fevers subsided,
cancers routed out with care,
spirits dispelled of their despair?

Why am I here,
not there?

I am my companion.

This is what I was meant
to learn bare.

In the beginning,
as at the start
of creating a separate self,
in the very act of love,
in the very midst of love,
some men kneel as if to pray
to lie
to die
to yield

Before
Above
With
Woman.

Possessing gifts unexposed
is my survival
is my loneliness
before windows
beyond windows:
liberated only by
an evolving identity
self image, my face
and its red leaf eyes of war.

These words here are a prayer,
now this side of the bar
of gifted hesitation, where
I pray for a long life for
my propitious wife
my ample bride,
the woman
who has been a window
on to my skillful doubts
my unbidden silence.
We Two together,
amphiscians casting shadows
on both sides of the sea,
are an unknown being,
an independent caring,
carefree elemental entity of One.

EVE AMONG THE LEVEES

Undiminished by time and knowledge,
my feelings run amok.
I prefer
          to back into the future,
          to keep my eyes plucked,
my vision afloat,
my selves eloped
to enlisted men of differing
nations, but an officer
spots me first, always.

Wondering where the elegance is
in a uniform, internally I'll search
eternally, imagining that all
          of the universe
          is already in my brain.
Because I am not the one
in this peculiar verse and universe,
I know that my mind, which is also
your mind, will continue
to remake itself.
How many have to die
before I—
before I live again
unknown forever?

An eternal beginner,
why should I think
back into a racial self?
Why do we narrate our way
back to a fall?

Why are my daughters in your book
never named at all?

ALWAYS WAR

Rising, I slip to the basin
To wash my face and drown.

Always war. Always money.
Money stokes war.
War breeds money.

Coming wakeful out of sleep,
Dowsing from fitful rivers,
I cross the red and white
Marble of my brain matter,
Searching on this off day
For a context, for a reason,
For the apparition shimmering
Just before the doorway.
Try as I might to hold back
The end of dreaming,
The start up of dawn,
The communion call to prayer
Wafers its way into my room.

Sometimes the light's not right
For my cataract eyes;
The sunlight, the room's light,
The moonlight, the wharf's lights,
The park's light, the night light,
The day light: whatever the moment
Offers I swallow to see clearly.
No moment ever rises empty
But some will feel so anyway,
Like a pause among notes rising,
Before the next beat descends,
At times a fist, a palm, a kiss.

After deep drowsiness, daylight
Knocks that way sometimes also,
Soaking through the curtains
Against an unconsciously slept

Room already over lit all night,
Now altered by eyes denied
The right light.

IN A SEMITIC CEMETERY

In Algeria, I once understood about cemeteries by their
Gravebed sculptured headstones that worship turns out
Personality and leaves the face formless, that a moment
Of concern is immortal but transitory: one lifetime, one
Meeting, a crossing over of private experiences; a return
To quantum gravity.

The cemetery is the strangest of men. The angriest
Of women. The soft inadvertent touch a baby extends
To the complicity of wind with leaves. A neatened
Reconstruction of an indivisible moment where perception
Twined around an earlobe's dimension is already a theory.
It is a defiant classification, a militant explanation, insistent
Generalizations. Compelling and grasping divergent
Directions into a singlemany order and gardened texture.

My own assumption, lacing the light of blood, conflates
Visions, sighs, and shudders of resignation tethering
Gravestones hemmed to the landscape's time and resolution.
I have come here today as always at the end of my stay, as
I have in Morocco, Tunisia, Turkey, Zanzibar: to understand.
Each city or island itself: Izmir, Lamu, Oran or Alger, whether
Berber, Arab, Jew, Muslim, or Christian, whispers a misunderstanding
God-forgiving intuitive distortion to me. Where there
Would be snow dusting the soil in winter, or endless
Rain soaking the earth in pools of mud, there was only
Dust settling like slush at our summer feet, the gateposts,
And the corners of our eyes. Herbs, spices, virgin oils nor
Funeral sandals could match the feudal hold of any city's
Fatal desires. Our thrust each morning into the surrounding
Square for breakfast before battle battling with bureaucrats
And bourgeois minions was premature. Unthoughtout, exhausted,
Expended, my own love for immediate history would no longer
Suffer idiots nor measure up to any civilization's indigenous
Lore. I all too soon could no longer receive nor spill upon a naked
Garden's floor native blood money, native fire, native passion.

Born of nations are things that die. Things that live rise.

TEAROSES AND PURSESTRINGS

But

    we

    during our   present juncture

    should clap hands   for an uprush of calm,

for the manyawkening   silences

of the moment   and its distances, of

the knowledge that   transformations

                        are an unbodying.

We need

    the curling   of evolution,

    the firstlast   greatbody

                        of drift

                        into

the ordinary now.   Vigilant

history,   the light that

bridges ,   soils under

and accepts   the apprehensive mileage

of an eventual   continuity.

I hear   the odor

of time   dim

                        then pulsate.

Aromas

    and darning   needles

    trowels   and plant dust

    smoke

midafternoons

evening   lawn sprinklers

                        curtaining the light

of endbegin   as we swallow

our face

for comfort   from a tin cup

cramp

the drowsy   liquefaction of the day

                        into mild departure.

Treacherous
    can be   a day
    the tendency   of our mind's
variable guesses.

                Authentic
                is
the adorationlust   light
of our grammatical   covenant.

                Be
but be a birth of hands
loving the everenduring   song moistened on my tongue.

My blood
    flows where   space convinces edges.
    My blood   flows luring borders
    and
if my face subsides and blooms again,
walling up a different form,
                remember the easy drift
the pinched moon   and to forget.

NOSTALGIA AND PREDICTION

Some time ago   In Chicago

As across the corridors day broke down, as across the city
Evening buildings withstood the heat and I pushed out
Revolving with the door into the street to enter not far away
The terminal that would lead me beyond the inadvertent city,

From ballet practice commuting homeward on the train,
In the perfunctory rain, spanned a young girl across our aisle,
With an absentminded smile, the tight adolescence of the evening.

I was struck how the true root of reduction gloats in dismaying
Dominion, in monumental ruins, virgin portentousness that men
And women claim they wish to be done with. Pursuit of innuendo
Coddles anonymity, as garish seawind distending the syllablethrilled
Tongue bruises speech, as stunning stillness in high-ceilinged mansion
Rooms brandish family portraits.

Amidst crycontacting gentleness, however, every life in its evolution
Is born to revolt, but there are some lives not worth living, soaring from
The right to revolution, the search for primary particles, where the stern
Drift of prevision crowds in, interferes with the way a building takes
Swaying shape, the way branchbending silence, rooting union, chases
Down drain spouts the bewildering urban rain.

But there are controlled explosions, beak to beak, paw to paw, petal
To petal, that make us go, retrieve to secrecy, into tampeddown
Etymology.

The earth is ceasing newer, evolving us back against the serene
Savannah of doom. This is our gift: to see already, to know
That those with single bodies will not know oneness, that in each
Of us spreads a stealthy seashore where the inherited ache of history
Lulls below a sly ganglion commanding our construction,
Our newly pinched retina. In a smooth, small stone the whole world's
Configuration blurs then renews.

The detail of sedulous quietude slits the golden seam of things,
The particles of root, the earthquake molecules of truth. Startled
By the texture of echoes, we greet, await, illumination then blinding.

Fascination often hibernates in the corners of drawers,
The depth of ashtrays, in the webbing connecting human fingers
Sprawling. Peering cloudward for the broadbosomed ship, we live
By daydreams among reeds long through the ages, one fist in the other,
In this keeping of our quiet clay.

The valves of life with no beginning, no ending, can stretch
To the reach of the river, adjusting necessary revelations,
Restoring necessary balances, pressuring day to seize the trees,
The roofs, the complexities of purpose, that our voices might
Not be eviscerated bells, stereomyopic, that a spiritual event
Manifesting a divine being might sprout the early glow of logic
In our throats, that illusion might transform our seeing.

ARMS ON FIRE

      Distractions not withstanding: alarm bells
going off in a parent's imagination, sirens
barreling across the city in the distance,
a ship's foghorn on the midnight river,
a rain's rhythm along night rails, the front
room television drowning out unwanted
disturbances, the bedroom radio whispering
lust into a moist, Blueswarming, ticklish ear,
as gusts of wind flatter dead leaves along
asphalt, pavement, ditches.
      A gun shot premature getting off everywhere,
going off somewhere unknown, and nearby;
too near surely to be a neighbor's instant,
lost scream, its sudden echo too far gone
not to hit home. In the city. Always in the city.
      I fell asleep with 4 children sickened by tainted
milk in China and woke up with 53,000. In the
nation. Always in the ancient nations. Deaths
rise in India from hurtling rains and exploding floods.
Stock market futures fall when America worries
over efforts to rescue its economy in free fall,
our limbs armed to the teeth with worry, fear, and anger.

AZALEAS IN RAIN

This is a letter. To you. But why
Do I need to identify it, committing
It here to memory on paper? Why
Not just start right in, as rain comes
Sometimes, unannounced by thunder?
Let it be what it is to be.

My thoughts inside are keeping time
With scattered outside showers. I worry
About your azaleas, because we haven't
Had much rain. It promises to fall today,
In the city as well as here in your inheritable
Southern northeast woods. These woods
Like this letter are for you.

I am the hesitant rain that should
Come to parent your azaleas. I will
Be your father forever.

KUAN YIN DESCENDING

Surrounded by bleached-hearted Americans, abandoned by
The hidden condemned unnamed, I felt left more equal in rage
And splits than one can ever recall. Pregnant as wives widowed
Through death, assaulted under false friendships, women, their
Boys and girls, cry out. Words falling spill out without navigation
In reams across, over, pages. Certainly, America will once again
Need books during these days of the crimesaddled "Merry Christmas"
   President to remind all the worlds to come of
   Ridiculed and slaughtered Martin and Medgar; of
   Asthmatic, herniated, hemorrhoidal Jacob and Li'l Guim;
   Whipped and scarred, scarred and whipped, enslaved
   Marianne; maimed Queto Manchot; "Idiot"-mocked Sery;
Roped and burned dangling Emmett Till from a tree; of spat upon,
Bruised John Lewis, bruised and spat upon; of Percy Julian's fired
Upon and firebombed home. Homeless country dust murmurs
more.
    We, every one of them us,
    Driver and driven,
    Slaughterer and slaughtered,
     Come again
     And again
    Chained in disharmony
By brainless, embarrassing, sniveling weasel smirks
Of craven politicians in search of unity, in disunity
    Created by
Indifferent pharaohs, caligulas, hitlers, trumps.
Who are we as we teach the Divine
    To become more human,
    To cease reciting to us
In cadences that shear the blood
Artery of the human heart;
    To gate in
The electromagnetic swirls of the waves of rivers
And the aorta's meaning?

Some things cannot be helped,
As there are also some people
    Mere decency cannot invade.

Standing and kneeling are choices, though not on the racist
Slave auction block that commanded standing. Nor on bended
Knees and bent ankles crumbled under the weight of inhumane
                    Blows to the human lower back
Where pain and aches persist today as baked in memories
                    From the ovens of yoked histories.

PUTTING SAD ASIDE

Entering our own Dark Ages, brought on by
Invasions from within, not without,
By religion's misunderstanding of science,
What should I say to the friend overharvested
By the spider of pneumonia, by the piety
Of influenza, bent by the architect of cancer?

Lying here on the floor on still another New
Orleans night, there on the sofa, or even in bed,
What could I believe in now and then instead,
But find there still more beauty later? Ten
Million were crushed in the first world war,
Forty million in the second. How many more next?

I love the sofa and the floor,
To spread beyond my body's flow;
Listening there to hear, reflecting
There to contemplate, looking inward
To see and to meditate.

Sad left, lifted some years ago, in 1992;
Abandoned, forgotten more likely. I had to
Be opened, opened up more by then. To redo
The personal spine's urgent endeavor;
To recognize the person spying
The murmuring asshole in others was
I observing me.

For friends can get lost forever.

When may, will, shall the chaotic,
Offputting fiction and simplicity
Of my contradictions cohere?

DRINKING

In coffee drinking Greece,
I drink tea,
And attend Liturgy as the women
Do, but from a bench in the square
Below the church doors and gates.

In tea drinking Turkey,
I drink coffee,
And attend Remembrance as the men
Do, but from a bench in the courtyard
Outside the mosque's doors and arches.

Sitting stock still in either dimension
And frame of mind, I eavesdrop,
Listen in, and grow warm and comforted
By memories, voices, and known yet
Unknown realms. My spirit emerges
From my body like a spontaneous self-coupling
Symmetry defying gravity and a vaulted sky.
Inside and outside, I contain open time.

From the café window burners of
Smyrna and Thessaloniki,
I sip the hot dark draughts
Of Izmir and Salonik
Swirling at my lips from handcrafted cups.

Around my neck hangs my camera.
At my fingertips rests my palmtop.
Each needs ever increasing knowledge
Of the human being to become more improved.
The camera: the eye; the computer: the bodymind.
The trusting eye, the self-centered, questing
Brain's antennae, desires to grasp more
And ever more sensitivity, resolution, and speed,
To teach the body to embrace its indeterminate
                    Immortality.
It's important to take chances.

Life, our first chance, is the greatest
Of narratives. Life is not
Worth the syllables without
Chance, necessity, and human design.
Voices in my head whisper, "Do
Something before it becomes too late.
Before time is reckoned as only benign."

GUESSWORK

The paths of travel will be personal and individual, and
We will be studying the entire universe from life to life.
I called her Diane, a Comeaway Bistro waitress, but she
Is Sighanne. She takes orders as her husband Noel
Draws drinks.

Perhaps I walked back into classrooms so as not to see,
Except for traveling back, that everything beyond my
Back and front door is changing. I called her Diane,
But she is a Sighanne.

I announced over several weeks that I had graduated
From the university, when I meant I had retired from it.
Am I entangling memories as my tongue travels my mind
As my mind travels my tongue unraveling matted fibers
With slips?

Some say there is life after death. I believe there are infinite,
Concealed worlds after death that matter most. Some artists
Can't do hands. Some render beauty in fingers caressing love
In a palm or hand resting on a knee or shoulder blade.

Gustav rattles our imagination now while Hanna humps his tail
Winds. Will they consummate their heat? Odds are she will
Cut tail and veer off toward the warmer Caribbean. Gustav
Short-tailed menaces our nerves. From all the downed trees,
If we go up from the land, we may not get back in. If we stay,
We may not get out. Hurricanes are guesswork for households.

Guesswork curling their oars and telescopes, Africa's, Asia's
And Europe's sailors hew, cleave, and cut through the currents
Of centuries toward the edges of their medieval maps.

We today warp unknown waves, reaches, and wraps, driven
By a hundred billion brain cells without a center, except for
The one we see in the mirror, exploring the center of known
And unknown beauty of the universe and of all the worlds.

Our best words have not been written yet. Where is my
Storyteller? Who is He, who has bitten off more than
We can chew at any one time? Who is She? Who is It?

Defined and distorted by words, as if all intuitive maps are
Illuminated at their edges with accurate ideal portraits
Of forms, universes, realms, groves, and beings, we sail on
Towards home, as if Jacob were shifting toward Yisrael,
Saul toward Paul, Yehoshua toward the Christ, Avram
Toward Ibrahim, Moses and Muhammad toward the Temple
And the Dome.

When the timelines are obscured, we always wish to be taken
Beyond our equations and scriptures to tease apart the grooves,
Seams, ruptures, sinews, ruffles, and fiber of incognita with
Science and Art.

"May I ask you a very, very, very personal question?" I
Asked out of panic as we strolled along the country road
Before landfall, as I diverted the conversation away from
Minatory hurricanes lifting their kilts, plunging their spiked
Heels, as they skipped and danced across the Atlantic. "No."
"Would your answer have been the same had I not used 'very'?"
"Yes." We walked on in our idle, diverted chat as Ike menaces
Florida and Josephine stepping off from Africa swerves across
The ocean toward the Caribbean shores.

As I looked out upon the faces of the freshmen I taught days
Before we broke class, rank, and status to escape the weather's
Menace, an exhausted sadness quickened the room, for they do
Not see, as Black Sea historians have taught, and do not understand,
That all lands belong to all their peoples and also to none of them.

Shepherds of many shapes in dark suits and earrings, enter our living
Rooms and hotel lobbies like moths emanating from the mouths of
Politicians vying to be better butterflies before their pastors and rabbis.
We lounge here and there in different rooms, wondering about neighbors
Separated by fear and survival of the separate self before rash
Earthquakes, hurricanes, landslides, imams, priests, and rabbis crash.

I often think about my childhood's indifference, my adolescent's
Insouciance. The woods rooting my memories are older than America's
First settlement or Annaba's bishop saint. The personality and character
Of Augustine, called Blessed by some, Saint by others, is all guesswork.
For all lands. Nostalgia, collecting the stain of memories, whether accurate
Or not, we are always explorers, immortal archaeologists, scuttling dead,
Saline floors of private lore just below swiftly moving currents topping
Our brain.

It is time we come out of hiding, putting aside capsized, hewned centuries.

GOOD PARENTING

My myth is that my desire to have owned my uncle's
Gift with his hands took root in you as your parents'
Blood rooted, too. I like believing that. I adore your
Mother for love's assistance to assistance. My uncle's
Brother possessed this gift exactly by desire. My Father
Was a good student of his brother; though I on the other
Hand, only an insouciant, inattentive one to my father
Once my uncle, a veteran, had died in hospital in Hot
Springs, Arkansas. I treasure and envy your optical and
Manual capture of art on canvas, in stone or paper, and
In the photographic moments possessing you. I love you
For you and for your enviable,
          Inviolable citizenship
          In the fourth dimension.

I praise your parenting me. You parent me well in the
Patient breeze of your presence of self, of the form
And structure of the day. You have me always looking
For everything new in the world, and I now see my
Mother and father and our ancestors behind every veil
Flowing out deep within every expanding cycle where
          Walls wall out and fall away.

The art around my father, cast in the sweet aroma
Of sweat, sawdust, and factory concrete floors,
Was his unmet dream to move us to Maryland,
Where he would farm, and to realize to money
Men, and phantom agents, his blueprint plan
Of an automobile that would run powered only
By water. A gentle man, and kind, he hardly
Talked much, except about both Roosevelts
And Adlai Stevenson. Like me, and now you,
He seemed to keep secrets. Disappointed
By his second Ford, he drove only Chevrolets
Until the day he died. Never sick a single day
In his life, he died in khaki pants and a plaid
Shirt. The funeral home never did return
His Elgin pocket watch and Masonic ring.

Buried in a grave site with my grandmother
Anna and my uncle Grover, he, they, survive
      There with Bertha, my mother,
      Our honorary historian,
      In my haunted brain.

Compulsions morph. We all after all, I now see, share
Gifts as form and heart exchange consciousnesses outside
      Different gates.

No presence ever loses. It is only the unseeing eye that
Envies random lint on the frayed black silk of Mary Queen
Of Scotts' slip or the cedilla hanging like a Gauloise from
Algerian Frenchman Camus' lips or Dalí's antenna moustache
Below foglight eyes as the worlds mandate upon us to be
      Like everyone else, which we must resist.
These days we sift aside pixels, not crumbs, to come
      Up on the larger picture.

A FUNERAL ORDER

Reilly has a closed gaze or look
That seems to be on the verge
Of innocence, even naivety.
Behind our plundering stealth
Of glances, when our own sly,
Insouciant examination shifts
Along her range of possibilities,
We finally arrive at our own
Naivety and realize we had been
Had. The evidence is in the smile
That seems to be no smile at all,
But only a gaze, a terrible patience
That waits for us to make fools
Of ourselves, then to move on
For the next in procession.

The farther away we stroll across
The room, the more her stroked lips
Defiantly seem to be a smile.
The closer we return, the more
Beguiling stone she seems.
I am no sculptor of such rock,
Nor a stoker of flames on canvas,
Nor a strummer of hymns on strings.
I dream of the music of murmuring
Rivers among mountains.

There she is again: photo-framed
On a shelf, ripening in the sunlight
Of our eyes' imagination. How real
Is she, laid out there, coffined
In velvet, hair coiffed in white that grew
Back late to fight and fence off the cancer;
Casketed like a deceptive treasure
Chest; chest, though heaved, unmoved?
O, dead breast, do you not know that
The single absolute
Is that all is relative,

Equally ridiculous,
Equally beautiful?
Our prayers there in the chapel ascend just so
Like incense and descend so like holy water sorrow

IZMIR

Here on any day of any August week
the heat screams our disgust in our meek
faces.

If I close my eyes, even behind
sunglasses, I can spy the traces
of this heat's blinding mind.

The sadistic sun's crimson orifice
bristles, beckons, and belly dances
among eye-aching whitehot spaces.

Too hot to avoid,
even through shut darkened eyes.
I rush under the shade and shadow
of pine trees nearby,
ripping off my undershirt
under the hot wind's drab lace.

Once again I am someplace
and do not know why, even though
I got myself here intentionally
In Front of the mirror's back.
Birds surely must know
when they are about to die.
We never see them

just drop from the sky.
I ought to look the science up.
With intensity.

From behind the mirror I
stare, gaze at myself,
brittle amidst tidal waves

of fractured contradictions.
Perhaps I'll never
understand what's going on

but will take a stab
anyway. With what am I
continuous that matters?
With matter itself,
he in the mirror might say.
I am not alone. At least

Life is a big bang,
the universe on a roll.
What I sense is this:
Where the soul contradicts
Science, soul's soul must change.
Somewhere along its threading net,
the brain surely must hold and rearrange.

IN BASRA

In Basra, wanton men roaming through streets
evangelizing law, pursuing women of their
private desire and public hatred, carry out their
threats, and with a hard on murder women using
makeup, or for what they wear.

On the women slain there and here they dare
to pin as excuses verses in holy script
revealed generations before, now days ago
scrawled by unholy hands pummeling
feverish ink across helpless, aged scraps of paper.
Ink, with the blood of women who will no longer diaper
young daughters and sons. Ink from impotent pens,
with the blood of women whose faces will no longer
reflect the faces of women of all religions. Ink
soiling the fingers of men who neither protect nor caress.
The gash such men prefer to gaze upon first no less
is the gash from knives, the sheepish sacrificial slit
across the throat, the hapless blood-soaked groove
of the stilled corpse. How women live, marry, and die
before the eyes of braying men is the shame of every age.
I wish, in holy different books, we could turn a page.

PHANTOM WILD AMIDST DOMESTICITY

There is always tomorrow in the City of Ambiguity,
          Which is now already today.
          I need sleep. I need tomorrow.
          The City wishes death away, forever.
The shadows and shades of night echo in.
I struggle to fall. Nothing engulfs me. Sinister
Whispers behind the curtains, the halls, down
The pipes from the flues in the walls, I hear
Footsteps and tiptoes from other rooms; from
          Rooms and the attic upstairs.
Some nights like this, I lift up from the sunken
Sofa because I can't take it anymore, walk to
The back porch door, discover it's only a soft,
Misty rain falling among trees and flower
Gardens below the moon. Or an aircraft's
Drone overhead. Through the night air, I
Drag myself to the porch swing, falling
Exhausted there to sleep until dawn.
          Then fall again below all imaging.
I don't like dawn. I sleep through the morning.
The day is half gone. Asleep through the morning
On the back porch swing, I dream of scheming night
Vines covering my whole pergola body, twining up my limbs
Beneath and through my skin like grape vines
          Rooted at my feet in space. I got so,
          I craved this lucid dream more,
Luxuriating in dreaming it over, over again. The more
I dreamed of vines, the more sweatsoaked dreams began
          Visiting me in empathy near morning
               Light and air.
During the dream now I feel pleasure and strength but
Once awake, ashamed and soiled, I've no one to put me
To sleep, to wake me, or to love me. In these woods I am
Armadillos who gouge my ground in the night near where
The pond edges the back woods, or feral hogs who trample
Through the woods among the trees.
          I fear swine fever or leprosy:
          Wild amidst domesticity.

VI. A GATEFOLD CELEBRATION

ANT ALGORITHM

I felt an ant bite in the afternoon today; the second one this
Week, actually. Up my path to the cemetery road to place
Garbage out, and a bit more up the road to the mailbox
Roadside, rolling the garbage barrel from under bamboo
Cover, as I edge the road to cross from the headgate.

Reaching into the tin box for my mail, I sensed the itch.
By the time I returned back to the house and made a quick
Phone call to some friends about meeting for lunch on Saturday
Two towns up, I noticed I had an ant bite between two fingers.
I first felt the stinging. Then I saw the red bump.

I suspect my dreams' kinship these days with this bite. A few days
Ago I ambled out on my land to sprinkle poison on a tremendous
Number of killer red ant beds dotted here and there on the mowed
Lawn near the house and surrounding gardens, and among the eight
Acres of trees. Taking mostly the whole of the afternoon, I started
From the wooded areas and made my way slowly forward toward
The road, zigzagging to wherever there ant beds might breed.

Their daring promontory beds seemed to be everywhere. I had just
About completed the full round of my assault when I spotted the mail
Lady slipping mail into my mailbox some yards up. I didn't want
Her to see me spreading poison here and there on the ground because
I had once asked her advice on the best way to rid myself of ants.
She encouraged me to spray dishwasher liquid on each bed. I tried
That. Nothing happened; it didn't take, or was working so slowly, I
Couldn't detect a difference:

But now here I was, spreading poison on the land, the very thing
She sensed I would not care to do. Otherwise, why would I have
Asked her for a non-poisonous method in the first place. It's like
This: we all know that at some point in the future our Universe will
Come to an end; and at some other point well before this end, the sun
Will simultaneously implode and explode asunder. Yes, there's plenty
Of time to worry about that, but it's a very worrisome thought ad infinitum.
I also know this day will end and tomorrow will come, and tomorrow
Will end, as the day after tomorrow will come, ad infinitum.

So I ponder: should I use dishwasher liquid, which will do the trick and take
An eternity or should I move now today, tomorrow, to put the little creatures
Down?

A LONEGOER'S LAMENT

If the death of my body could be seen,
It would seem in slow motion,
Separating from the love of somebody
Too bashful at times to be named,
As, touching the world in my mind,
I think on her
And of when our hands
Were so unnew to be the whole room:
        The wind crawled meaty in mind toward Aïn Draham
        Across the Mediterranean at Tabarka,
        Took shape in her still dress and sand,
        And in this squat and wordless room
        The curtain lapped my face from jerky sleep.
        I breathed the room undressed;
        As if curtain had become eyeful and windblown,
        Sensed my stomach sucking breathless against the bone
        Where fingers might have nudged.
        Feeling sulked in at me,
        Gripping handless on pain and memory
        Of seagulls coming in low at us,
        Dipped in their own wings, then
        Sweeping out above the broken bridge resting in sea water
        Under the sun going down in the last suck of the mountain.
        I rose halfway,
        Lifting the window in my eyes,
        Watched dawn break sore and bare:
        Perhaps bruising against buildings,
        Dangling downslope or
        Scattering in leaves
        Green and black. A seabird cawed
        From somewhere off in memory without suggestion,
        But dawn and seabird were nothing
        But the curtain flapping back, back,
        Back on the surface of my eyes, deeper within
        My body throbbing to trace a hint of female form
        In the curtain swelling and blowing
        In the feeling of the wind.
        Room strained under echo in mind

Of children in yelling games
And I screamed within my own head
To put my quieter self at rest: as if *scream* had
Swarmed from the toil of darkness into
My eyesight as my own face,
Openmouthed and quenched in depthless swallow
Of my own voice.
I felt
The room undone,
And felt
A foolishness of my own skin in the wind
And felt
That laughter and hunger had not been born.
Her briefly leaving was like shadows
Where there is light
Or like shadows
Where I might bloom
Without the soil of her loins,
Aggravating the birth of death
With a light in my eye.
I have breathed an air that was flesh,
Sensed a change in sense,
Found I would live by daydreams
Long into an old man among reeds
With one fist in the other
In this keeping of my quiet clay.
Not even the moment of a city's growing
Satisfies the downward thrust
Of silence bulldozing sound and ground elsewhere
In my brain.
No green thorn as fresh as a face
Will open me up to change as young
As dying roots in renewed ground.
For we men together
Have moved
Through woman,
Woman's merely
Imagined passing
Our dying.

ANGELS AT MID DISTANCE

My city died, drowning.
We had always taken a bath before, from one season
to the next, with or without a hurricane. Inundation
was everyone's middle name. "Hard showers" was
what we called heavy rains that wouldn't let up. On
the local weather channel or in other cities all the time,
they said "thunderstorms."
But this time was different. This one was different.
Whole neighborhoods floated away, forever. The Law
and the Army kept us out, at as much of a distance as they
could muster. We snuck back in after three weeks, the
three of us, to peek, to know, to understand, to evade the
insult of being kept at bay from one's own possessions
and property. The nation was at war then, an unwanted war
willed like foul weather by our own Prince of Chaos.
We entered unrecognizable neighborhoods at the crack
of dawn, the new light of a new day still behind us. This
ride was no joy ride this time. This was something different
this time. Nothing looked familiar, except for the visions;
though even they were different this time.

I have always had visions. Spirits and angels are my constant
companions. They are always there for all of us, in fact; but not
everyone will notice them. I am not egoistical, so I don't assume
I am the only one who can spot them, though I've never heard
anyone speak about seeing them out there, in the middle distance.
Perhaps I am being egotistical.

Angels and spirits are constantly with us, crossing their own
miles. When I first understood that, as a young boy, I no longer
choked up at seeing them floating or soaring by on wings; they
Often turned to gaze at me as they passed on. But only the angels
Smiled as they spread their wings even wider. Spirits would glance
In passing, passing on. Passing on, angels smiled. But this time,
After the hurricane, the spirits did not look my way, but hung their
Heads, slumped into their many wings, as if in mourning. The angels,
Their wings clutched, glanced and would not smile, but farted.

Now, thinking back on that first dawn crossing back over the city
limits, I bite my lip, not to smile or chuckle, because that time, this
very time even unto now, was and is a mournful, beastly haunting.
The stench is still with me. Not the angels' smell, but the tepid,
Drying stink of the city's rotting away. The angels' scent was
The whiff of lavender or of sandalwood, as always. But they had
Never farted before, not audibly at any rate. I don't want to analyze
Any of this. I'd rather you do that, so that you'll have something to say.

WHY WAR

The Japanese War. The War with Japan. The Korean War.
The War with Korea. The Iraqi War. The War with Iraq.
Strange expressions, these.
But though we may say the War with Germany, we never
Say the German War. Why not? Is this racism? Does our
Language protect Caucasians? And why is it as if it is always someone
Else's war? Why isn't each of these wars called An American War?
And then there's that crazy preposition "with," as if a war
Is a dance with someone.
"May I have this war?"
"How about the next one, then?"
"I would like to relax a bit before I get up and war again."
"Fine. Sit this one out. I'll war around a while with others
And come back to you later."
War Room. Dance Floor.
War: the other courting ritual.

And what of poverty? Poverty changes everything.
But no one says, The Poor War.
Or: The Poverty War.
Though I have heard of the War on Poverty.
Poverty undermines everything and all of us because it's
Everywhere.

It's the one war we pretend to care about but never wage. We
Certainly can't coin the phrase The War for Poverty. Remember
"The War for Peace"? Because that would mean that we wish
To engage more poverty, which is what we must wish anyway,
Since we coquettishly avert our eyes whenever we sense it near,
Breathing down our pants or up our skirts, so to speak.

A person's flaws, or her or his one chief flaw, is not
As significant as the origin and seat of the flaw. There is,
Indeed, the Flaw. But its Origin and Seat are what we need
To scrutinize more. This should be our one abiding antinomian
Prelapsarian scrutiny.

A battle has an end and a beginning; a war, a lengthy
Legion of battles, does also, but hate speeches, revolution,
Insurrection, terrorism, sectarian violence, police action,
Military action, regime change, peacekeeping vigilance,
And the aftermath of war, such as the legacy of landmines,
The incursion of weaponized chemicals: each can last
Justifiably forever. We are competent at justifying armed
Insolence against our own human nature.

        The War with Human Nature.
        The Human Nature War.

        No, that will never do.

DISCOMFORT AND PLEASURES

Why Parker preferred sleeping on the divan beneath a window,
closed shut in winter, of course, and raised, of course, in summer,
the satin sliver curtains always drawn—she never understood.

She did sleep that way, though, by fooling herself. She'd read
each night sprawled there; sometimes a book, but every night,
two newspapers. Well into her reading after two hours or so,
she'd stretch out, to relax more, always almost promising herself
she'd go straight to bed once she really began to feel sleepy.
   Then she'd fall asleep straightaway. There.

   She slipped through the seams of sleep, seamlessly.
In her sleep, traditional formal boundaries blurred. Wakefulness,
drowsiness, and sleep slipped into the space and form of one another,
with the slight hint of personhood: three persons in one intermediated
   dreaming brain.

Sleep is a screen-saving activity behind which other things turn on
live. Her body, internal voice, and mind become interlacing media.
We know very little about such phenomena, not until a person wakes
up, and we get to question her, to drill her endlessly. But if the dreamer
never speaks of such an experience, and lives alone as she does, we are
not only dumb to further investigation, we are not even privy to the fact
that we could be on the edge and verge of a breakthrough scientific inquiry.
So the question of who the true interpreter of dreams might be never comes
   Up.
   Philosophers, poets, and scientists
have suspicions about dreaming. They suspect that the bodymind
brain in dreaming casts backward, further back than thought, and
forms a kind of national, linguistic consciousness, whose hypertext
templates act like the pages of a tome ruffling backwards in the wind
of a storm or the breeze of a warm day. Most night dreams act out
in daylight. Eons ago, Parker might have been Amatheia, a Nightingale
Sea nymph, rearer of life in deep Mediterranean waters; or Dione among
Gods; or Oshun, Goddess of orphans, intimacy, and diplomacy,

In bondage, when she dreamed, she dreamed she was overwhelmed
by the ardent descent of sultans; overcome by the amorous embrace

of an Indian of the American West; kidnapped, once when ponderously pregnant, by a Dravidian warrior. In her sleep she never felt the hope of rescue, nor of a redeeming ransom forthcoming from a forgotten Malian lover.

Whenever she recalled a dream the following morning or later on in the day, she would often daydream, fantasize, about possessing, or being possessed by, the cruel power to inflict disproportionate pain on her captors. Skinflailing was the favorite method that she forced her mind to imagine, but somehow she could never shear a captor's body down below his waist. The territory seemed frighteningly unfamiliar to her. Obviously, her dreams of bondage were, though real, unrealistic.

> She always stopped at the waist,
> then shook herself away from her
> fantasy: retreat from, not resurrect
> into, the slumbering arms and waist
> of a Malian lover.

IN BEAUTY'S EMBRACE

With binding laughter,
time's rich, teasing silences
awaken in me,
        disappearing trifling thoughts
        where I am never wounded.
Fully alive now
in the thresholds of my blood
infusing my limbs,
        corrugating the soul's bones,
        calling me forth to be one me;

in beauty's embrace
calling me to be myself.
Who am I really?

How can I expand the moat
ancestors and haters dug?
Trenches I have crossed,
in different dress on far shores,
greeted in the squares,
braced by the soul of my soul
and the wisdom of circles.

LIVING, BREATHING OUT

Where I do not hurt,
In the shadows of her eyes,
My lens on my country's life
Shapes a eulogy on its good thighs
Swaddled among loins of words
Alert as daybreak.
I will go down there
Broken as a bone
And rip it out, all alone
In the brazen muck
Rising toward my groin,
From the rustic rectitude
Of country ground
Where, with any luck,
Light falls out.

Light from light,
I'll whistle my way
To the end of the tunnel
Thrusting upward
Toward the opening
Of the nation's summit,
Where a bit blind I'll bow
To my and Earth's shadows.
I often wonder which world
We lost and which one we
Are losing now? How
Can we find our way back
Or forward, inside a mediated
Reality inside Reality?

With only one glove on
And one knee-high boot,
I have arrived looking for
An explanation from thieves.
Mine is a bass guitarist's
Personality trying not
To master, but merely

To learn to play the lute.
To find it everywhere,
I need the will of honey bees.
Rested, we linger untroubled,
Charmed by terror's glisten
And by the shame of the age.
The name of the power to hear,
Understand, believe, and listen
Is lost, soul embodied in a cage
Unfree. Where is it, I ask, unguided
By something to chew on, bumble
Bees trapped in my throat? These
Days women and men fall battledressed,
Accorded no time for a final salute
          Or sailboat.

MERE WAVE, TIDE, CURRENT

Mere wave, tide, current.
Mere electricity, water.
Mere blood, tears, sweat.
     In whomever rage resides,
     dealt idolatry abides.
No need to bend knees.
Because even anger, all
actions, are divine.
     Unjustifiable
     are all human words and deeds.

The breath from heaven's
maw animates herds, ponds, creeds,
with intense leaven,
     without discrimination,
     for the benefit of all.

At each cloud or wave,
cicadas sharpening saws
beneath brush behave
attuned to the ocean's laws
of unkind benevolence,
     snuffling across
     unsuspecting unwise land,
     where pleasure and grace
without creation's nestling
in one another's rustling
     embrace
     in haste.

SEPHTEN'S MISIDENTITIES

At night before sleep
overtakes me
or at times during a day,
when work does not
distract me,
  I repeat your name,
  my beguiling city,
  and my own name,
  Sephten Jealous Sit,
  to myself
  so that the heart's
  remembering
  can replace the tongue's
  loquacious remembering;
a percussive murmur of blood
replacing
a sigh or whisper
or taste.
  Some chuckling confuse me with Snatchmo
  because of his boastful love of art's love of
  women captured sculpted inside our museum's rooms
  in belladonna glory in nightshade on
  canvas, in photos; and outside in smooth,
  glistening metal or sparkling stone statues as
  he escorts visitors out to the city's Sculpture
  Garden to revere, adorate, nature's light in the day.
    Some think me Cimarron because
    Of his love for Antepli baklavah
    And Greek honeyed yogurt.
Every day is
a renewal of memory,
an evasion of nostalgia.
My voice creates you
and, in knowing you,
reveals you,
as a shadow its light.

> Your presence reveals me
> and, in knowing me,
> creates me,
> as a light its shadow.

Your name dwells
at the crossing's perfume
from shadow to light,
from throat to heart.

Often when I speak
This way, some mistake
Me for Phantom.

VEILS

On your way downstairs next time
Conspire to champion the light
In your red scarf and green dress.
       As you glide in and out of the lit air.
       As the sun negotiates the picture
       Window. Stop there, turn, stare,
       Then gaze at me, your frame aflame.
Heal my bellyaching. Convince me to
Place no shame at the feet of memory.
I don't know if I can stand going old.
       In my mind I picture myself staring
       At you across the room: You are old
       There. A refractive error, no doubt. I
       Am sure light entering my eye bends
The right way. Though I can see only
My back in the easy chair, I sense I am
Fading, too: a saddened old finally come. A
       Three-fingered death down my throat.
       Back and forth I run our years through
       My skull, our tears, our smiles, our veils,
       Cascading nails of my imagination.

AT WIT'S END

The fruit, a rare being that desires
To be eaten, signals its readiness
By changing color, so that it may
Sow its seeds spat from our delicious
Mouths, bequeathing its wisdom
Bite by bite to woman, man, and child.

What animates your icon in my soul
But the silk swirling disciplined folds
Of your dress capturing color,
Separating, meeting, claiming
Surrounding suggestive space
In the room, in my brain, in my heart,
In my aging intact entrails.

This is religion, our yoked contact
With one another, with outside forces,
With the universe. We do not stop
At the ends of fingertips when we extend
Toward one another but flow beyond grace
Into the immolation of unordered spirit,
Transfigured, illumined but for seconds.

DRY THROAT

Resorting to force at will,
Human civilizations are short-lived.
Baffled, I never know when our child
And I will disagree. Neither the cause
Nor the content, but only the effect,
Leaves me unrevealed: despoiled,
Pillaged of furthering new words
Emptied of other moments
In their goodness now forgotten
In my dry throat.

In the furnace of the raw belly of these
Notes nestle the insistent strings of our
Child's analytic musicianship on my soul,
Strumming into me like a liner note on
Our love; she a critic of my distractions
And the easy wanderings of my mind,
A harmony to the chords of my inattention,
Tweaking melody into the cadence of
My aimless missteps that I can neither hide
From her nor cease. A reminder, a teacher
Of note to my careless selves.

SO MUCH KNOWING

Once as an autumn evening quietly quilted
The street and sidewalks, I overheard her,
As we stood at a distance from one another
Outside a political book rally, affirm to someone,
 "You see that man over there—my father—
I got my love of books from him!" Did she want
Me to hear? Another time, during hurricane
Season, in storm-soaked words spat from fierce
Trembling lips, she fussed, "I know many things
You taught me. But now it's time for me to teach
You. You don't know everything, you know!"
What is it I am not supposed to know?

She has been a proud woman for quite a long time;
Since she was born, in fact (Everyone spotted
It instantly!). When I say "my child," "our child,"
I never mean an immature, obedient being, but
A petal from a rose, a blossom from a strong imperial
Magnolia tree, a cresting wave from the sea, a gust
From swift winds, an ordained egg in passing cloaked
By insouciant sperm swirling homeward.

Her syllables in anger and praise spilling
Over her lips like pomegranate seeds
Rejuvenate my soil, much like our tiffs,
Debates, differences, agreements renew
The driven drift of joy. So many questions
Chain-bang my brain.

How can the human heart just halt
And leave all of beauty behind?
Why is it impossible to heighten beauty
With another word: more-beauty?
How can my heart knowing beauty
Know when to shut off, down, cease

Into dry gristle?
How can I come here into this world
And want to leave it so loved?
How can I come here and meet you
And want to leave you so loved?
What can I bargain and barter with
For more life, more days, more years,
More beauty, more song?

How can I not even know me again?

Will she sit with her father's ghosts
Or her mother's first? We are three
Lives. I can't bear their end, nor
The story before their end, surviving
In family portraits and framed snapshots
In perhaps antique store baskets, before
Someone sits with the ghosts of her ghosts.
I should perhaps move away to barren land,
Sit somewhere else
Found a town there to rename after myself
To be remembered.

Prop me at the edge of the sand dunes of
Morocco, where my senses may drift out,
Becoming atoms again in the embrace of
Gravitas and quantum gravity.

Shall we reawaken urgently together again
From the Chaos swirling beneath the filaments
Of our brain and ritualize and manifest our unified
Anatomy, as we did once to create her? Shall
We emerge again as one, we three, as one will,
Manifesting every spike and hammer, every
Beam and socket? Love embattles us three
Gently enough so that we are neither defensive
Nor overwhelmed by it.

When I am dying, will I snuffle out on my back,
My stomach, on my side; my right side, my left?

Or will I be afoot, upright, staring off across the
Pond through the kitchen window, into the woods,
With my reading glasses in my hand; or in an easy
Chair on the veranda? These tosses and turns,
These switchbacked thoughts, visit me nights as
Altered images that I see in the rivalry of a mirror
Dim with dust and damp.

Glance. Gaze. Stare. The root memory of the eyes
                    Open.

SOUTHERN IMMORTALISTS

The amount of song
in a canoe is forever.
I know because of the mornings
the sun's conversation has spieled
across the edges of our eyes
and we, dewspoored with the
episodes of wild light, have sprinted   .
our skiffs along each new thigh of dawn.
       We had to go up.
       The waters are a great bringing up,
       and then the star wave energy.
       Immortality is death after death.

Some of us, no less than human,
the internal hunters, would
lag about, drag about, kick and scorn,
but the waters would renew us anyway.
And then the hum among startorrents.
The clucking of the hens through grass
held our sway no more than the bellyaching
ape clenching our hearts. We around
us should always see the truth of what
we say roundabout, not the reality of the sayer.
       We are what we be, with all its attachments,
       precursors whispered through to the next end,
       in our great softvoiced humanity,
       having grown wings with hands to trace
       the social and individual spoor
       of our honey bee heritage.

THE VANISHING POINT

A benefit of summers is that thinking assumes a different shape.
One question Charles Baudelaire and Salvador Dalí had every summer
As it grew hotter here by the day was, Who will be the next stranger they
Will meet? Whose universe will slip into his poem or on his canvas as a husk
Of influence, a lust of voluptuous defeat?

Whatever we do or not, *that* is our destiny: that doing or not.
A destiny always already achieves what can never be reached. Our
Destinies can be reached only by others as they perceive us as
Themselves in front of our backs toward the horizon at the vanishing
Point. I seek my memory for extremes among friends of my past to
Find what balance lacks. Either there is no reason at all or a reason we
Do not understand.

Reckless along the highway toward home, as I plowed
The pavement faster than usual and seduced away the hazard of
A swerve, the parallel gold and yellow reflectors guiding, tracing,
The dark road mirrored the pewter path of night in mid air as a gold
And yellow belt.

Our brains dangle along every vector across every world
Offering benedictions. Don't mock the monster, as children are taught
The lingering hatred in others' heart.

I grieve the mad man or woman, the one attracted by God,
Whatever that means, not the panicked one who has lost the way.

PEPSI TO COKE

Adorating the essential, elemental
Law of the original, eternal, universal
Teaching,

I prefer Chicago to New York,
Stevens to Eliot, Pepsi to Coke,
Gramercy Park to Old Town,
Hydrox to Oreos, Rhythm and
Blues to Heavy Metal, Blanton's
Bourbon to any other cask or kettle.

Abram
            on every page
Muhammad
            at the mouth of a cave,
Buddha
            under a tree,
Christ
            in the Garden of Gethsemane

Enter the opening way, the expansive
Bend in the path, and disappear, and
Come again the back way, along the
Side trail, off track, among companion
Women and men enjoying Barq's Root Beer.

I prefer raw silk to tentative remnants.
What was there about the way she touched
Me? Was her feather duster sweep at my
Shoulder a light finger ushering me toward
The restaurant door or was it a hidden,
Deliberate timidity to get to you? Was it
A surge of frightened self-revelation or
Nothing, just nothing, at all but my sudden
Next-day imagination?

That's what happens when we are some
Near-stranger's guests for dinner. One

Never knows what to expect and does
Not think or suspect until a very late day.

Was she confessing to me or apologizing
Because she wanted you?

VII. TIDES OF MIND

BLOOD

I long to walk in rain along city streets
          Midday for hours.
Imagining myself insular, isolated, holy,
Unique, and separate from the prickles
And trickles of mankind's blood horrors.

The stereotyped reviled by the privileged
Is like the left breast we see in paintings
          And photos of nude
Goddesses and contemporary women: it's
Always that smaller one that we see
          Then do not see
          And not notice.

This is still not a gainer's century to feel a friend
          Of Jews.
Like Blacks, hardly anyone's companion, they
Are never completely there; perhaps noticed,
But not seen. The generation no longer dragging
Through centuries of others' baggage has not been
Spermed and egged yet and they can never ever be
          Complete
          In their Friendships,
          And are despised for that.
Haters are the problem: Racists, The Anti-Semites,
Hitlers, Ayatollahs All. Especially the closeted
Ones with belated, always ill-timed, confused
          Puritan smiles.

About Blacks, they complain of an imagined greed
          For unearned entitlements.
About Jews, they scoff about an annoying
          Yearning for privilege
          Beyond blood.

          They scowl toward both
Or snuff a guffaw back behind equivocating
Lips. Such mouths are a lost theology, a withered

Economy, a moribund civilization, that will,
Of course, be reborn elsewhere again and again.
It's a matter of perspective, of course, where
Perception and perspective join in an artful
          Dancing away,
          Like oil and water
          Circling down an eddy.

How incomplete like desire passionate hate is.
For racism, bigotry, Anti-Semitism are always
Tinged with an erotic sip at the hater's lips,
A rush sifting through a reluctant lover's skin.

Their admiration can be found mostly in museums,
Chatting beneath their breath how an artist, a Jew,
Has captured precisely isolated Black limbs
          In marble, onyx, or ebony.

We long to learn and one day will of how
Soma testing has revealed their diasporic DNA harboring
          Black and or Jewish cousins' blood row.
          Eve beginning in Africa, Adam rising
          From beneath her ribs:
We--
Taoist and the asleep,
Jew and gentile,
Muslim and infidel,
Christian and sinner,
Buddhist and unawakened--
Are all One Drop now.

PHOTOGRAPHS

I often wonder whether bearing a child
Is a practice only of the mind for men as
It is a practice of the body and mind
For women? I never would have thought
Before knowing you that I would have
Gladly birthed you myself. Will you
One day become a bearer of bearers?

Purging our emails of old conversations
Is heartbreak enough. I am now my father,
Who never saw enough of me, he felt.
You are like his offspring, springing off
Among the firmament, a hand already dealt.

Am I writing to you or about you?
Am I waking from sleep or falling?

I never see you often enough for me,
Although I've your photos everywhere:
The window sill where my work table
Stands, where I've got three; a living room
Hall, a painting of a much younger
You there on a bedroom wall, and, of course,
In my wallet. Come to think of it, they
Are all of a younger you. You at an age
When I used to make up stories, of sage
Rain that cleared and dried up instantly,
Of grass that never overgrew; of lands
Of brave, magical little girls who could do
Anything and could do no wrong because
Their parents loved them long with the only
Kind of ferocity that was useful and necessary.

I now know beforehand that our occasional
Lunches will be quick. So I, evasive, work
My food around the edge of my plate,
Play and pick at it as if I were a younger you,
As if plate and food were photographs out of focus,
As I sift for clarity.

QUANTUM IMMORTALITY

Not dying
some finite number
of times constitutes immortality.

Perhaps
this is why we have war.
Death preserves ensuing universes looming off.

A mixture of waves,
my consciousness moves out
as interacting possible outcomes.

At our deaths
we split, we live,
forever surfing parallel waves.

Winds of history, waves of feeling, shudders of thought
vaulted and wooded,
flow.

SNATCHMO'S RIFFS

Red Ruby in the springtime.
We are the riffs in one another's measures.
A brother of my soul recalls his Rocky Top
woman who can stroke small things large.
Perhaps he will not mind when I take a sip
of ruby wine as I stroke Red Ruby's fingertip.
We are the riffs in the measures of nations.
Versed, we drum, strum, hum, sing.
Red Ruby in the springtime.
We say Red Ruby because her scars rooted
so deep perk up like rubber bands and worms
scrawled around her chin and cheek. When
she laughs her special smiles and coughs
away her grins, her trauma transfers to us
like second-hand smoke because we were
not there to protect her black skin from
assault in narrow daylight.

I pretend they are arrow beauty scars of the Akamba.

Red, Red Ruby!
In the springtime.

That was many notes back when our women,
Rudy's and mine, understood our need to rut,
to visit Rudy's Ruby in the springtime, when
her almond tree and tulips blossomed. But

They tell me that Ruby does not exist.
That she and Rudy are traces of my imagination.
That this is my way to combat for women a world
Philosophy that says:
            Put the vagina in jail.
            Wrap the vagina in a veil.
            Enclose the vagina behind lock and key.

And that Rudy and Ruby do not exist.

WAR

Wars are won, war is not. Stupidity
Of self molds an ailment in present time
On earth and pursues the cell's contumely:
A private, pathological end rhyme.
Some foreign land will blot the skies with suns,
Embedded intervals, disorder, behind
Computers calculating guns, and the planet's
Flesh corrupting loneliness.
        Over the hump of our being resume
        The volcanic, nested sores of the past;
        Courageous fears our blood, soil consume;
        It seems that our choices do not last.
And we must pretend an eternal call,
Plotting hierarchies of ancient fall.

HEPHAESTUS, FORGER GOD

Each created, engineered object has its secret pride:
                    Moons questing farther earths,
                    Inner screams as scattered occasions,
                    Yestermorrow's shadowlight,
                    That the city settling before our eyes
Each evening like a widening wound
                    Pulsates toward the center
                    The heart
                    Of a world of ignition I cannot imagine
                    Without autonomic intelligence.
                    Vehicles and humanoids on wheels
                    Crisscross the veins
                    Of my eyes
                    Of my mind's intentions
                    Of the holy city's limbs
Toward the semen sun drowsing at the intimate end
                    Of another street.
                    The day has come and gone
                    With the squealing, buckling drags of the subway
                    Shifting like a bug into night,

Worm into butterfly.
                    Cityside walking lulls my mind around,
                    Downtown the streets lamp up,
                    Uptown the rivers flow down
                    At night as thick watered silk,
                    Whispering to me that my children will go out

As the lamps at daylight.
                    But I would like to draw tight the blinds
                    Of the heavens against the dawn of their wheezing
                    And turn up the lamps of laughter
                    And forge the smiles of nights
                    Across the hearts of shadows
                    And grin past mechanical suns.

DOCTORING, HEALING

I have trimmed forth
Two before but am astonished
By the cardinal duality of life.
       Always, as in a long, longer time ago,
       Somewhen the walls of this or that woman's cave
       Chattered grin by slither, my brain,
       Two fists under bone, has sought to soothe her hilt
       In calm delivery and writhe up cool and warming
       Her birth of twins.
At times as these I feel that the female shape is an unfolding,
An embrace over man's riverrush; times when I,
Like some institutional manhandled beast, must coax
Another from her bowels; envying times that I want
To kiln my own and lift it out molded and cooling
Forth. Twice.
       But I, female and allgone twice over,
       Nurse only the waiting room of my mind
       And wonder of love of self and of love of self's self,
       Doctoring others' roots and fruit,
       Sprucing up another's bodytree of life.
       Though each smile delivered my way
       Does seem to requite my trained expectancy.

MZEE

Part Negro, part Indian, part Jew, part
Arab, I seldom go out to sessions on art,
Or in gatherings of any kind to deliver
Or receive curbed words from prisoners
Of niceties. There are too many mirrors,
Not all backed with silver.
            I am envious of young men who
            only in secret will have me in their
            company, without concealing
            their beauty, or in deference to my
            wispy gray hairs; or in some idiotic
            pretense seeming to be already grown
            up and ready to decay in a groaning
            groin of radicalism.
I'm very much against the tyranny of age.
            Women want me to be
            their fathers and, worse,
            their granddads, and me
            without a child to my name.
As if I'm not still learning
The way of the world,
The young men, they pretend
To defer to my wisdom.
But I would settle for an egalitarian friendship
            where they behave like my peers,
            as if they don't know they are much smarter
            and brighter than I ever was at their age,
            as if I'm not still learning the way of the world.
            The odor of disgust rises up my nostrils
            down to my throat onto my tongue.
            They need a yoking Middle Passage chocking.
What they naturally possess, we in our decay
Long for but unlike us, speaking of pensions
At 25 and Caribbean cruises, they do not long
For what is undone and revolutionary.
            They have not learned my lessons
            from Mama of 96 and others from
            her generation, in protection,

running from room to room,
locking every door, slamming shut
every window, pulling every curtain
before their eyes against the Bogey Man
in bushy hair,
magnificent beard,
Byronic collar,
and ocean blue beret,
imploring
"Marvelous! Marvelous!
At last your dream of
Dreams has come true!
You must go with me!
Where is your father?"

RECKLESS KNOWLEDGE, VIOLENT MEMORY

The leisure
some of us have
to take in the triumph
and harmonies
of a single moment's
implications
often gives our lives
an air of over determination,
an eternal immutability
threatening to disappear;
and a loss of spirit,
a perpetual mutability,
as if blood had drained
and transfused,
drained and transfused,
through a riddled body.
This is more so today,
every day even,
a loss of contour taking hold
in all the rooms and halls of
exhibition in the museums of
our lives; or among the dusty
nail bins of corner hardware
stores leaving the scene
forever.
A grove of sheep,
a flock of cedars
on a sloping, curving hill;
the slowed down fussing
of veiled bodies in intuitive spaces.
What have we lost
but the pastoral yearnings
for the ancient,
the timeless
experience
and newfoundland possibilities.
A pure perception
of matter in form,

a passing beyond
category, subject, genre,
becoming completely, totally,
provisionally improvisational,
human by immediately becoming
self.
          How possible
is the modern without
lawlessness:
corruption, denial,
cowardice, hypocrisy,
delusion, betrayal,
criminality, brutality,
lewdness, abuse, envy,
greed, jealousy?
          The only ones
laughing and giggling,
but mostly to themselves
and to ball players on the screen,
are old men, their sour groin perched
upon their sofas of pain.
          But the ancient
never starts first,
beginning only
after barbaric ignorance
in the latest evening wear.
          Threatened,
we will destroy the earth
and the abandoned soil
of sorrow will green again.

SILENCES

Silences
and a pair of startled eyes
are disastrous to marriage,
a pathology in the heart.
Women are victims
in all wars, and in peace
go to pieces flake by flake.
Flail by flail. Attachment
Is their undoing.

Somewhere the world over,
in a valley, on a mountain,
along the dark alleys of cities,
the amber ditches of towns, in
any number of tents and national
hovels and bowels, there are invisible
or vanished women forgotten.

This is you and not me,
my eyes-averted Readers.
You are making this all up
as you listen, to tell you the truth.
Listening, you will also understand.
Nothing is ever inherently obvious.
Everything begs a retelling.

When the impulse and free fear
to flee from your flesh transforms
the nostalgia for days of mulberries
and slumber, of green and black figs
and passion, into a percussive
though benevolent amnesia, what
choice will you have but escape?
Or stay. Just stay.

The escapades noted in concupiscent diaries,
tussled now in memory, rendered malignant
by time, forgetfulness, and scuffed lies,

narrate self-serving nostalgia among motherless
sons, fatherless daughters, among scuffled
generations.

THE ULTIMATE SYMPHONY

There is perhaps this shadow that we must pursue,
Eye its imposture of bony poise,
Stroke with hands hesitant around noise
Its final sigh, the soaring out of its ultimate crew.

There is this rose song that we, slumbering
Along strings universal, must regather,
Emigrate among its thorny whispers
Toward its burning, turning crisis,
Scan an ineffable, bountiful spacebough of chant
Where sometimes only gesture suffices.

There is this mist whose visions we must imagine human:
Silence seeping until the slow heap of silt
Claims the tideënding lake, fireflies dueling
After dusk until railway dawn glints
Across ancestral crafts.

There is this light, yes, this light whose
Crude matter we must absorb, scraping
Inside the recondite flames of sheathed
Soil toward the past,
Its rays barbarously loyal.

There is perhaps tomorrow, kingdom of sculptures,
Trough of storms, that I must produce, soothe
With batteries at my wrists the lamps of your
Fractures, when I must wire your visions
In summer storms manumitted.

No. Do not move motionless out of sight.
No. Do not stand on my hands.
Fit the tool of our rock desire
To the grasp of humanity's pebble fire
That we might come here without
Doubt, sow this mosaic across the land,
Breathe and feel our accurate sigh
From within swelling out.

Out of pain, out of knowledge,
When I hold silence aside,
Unearthing thought, shoveling time,
And lineless words abide; when
I muscle birth around my wrists,
Grip the light bulb overhead,
Squeeze it gently, connecting
Flesh to housewire, living room
To attic, linoleum to window pane,
And manacle outward to visions
Beyond midair where the urge
To journey bare is bred. There is some
Symphony of energy that we,
Gatefold immortalists, carnal archeologists,
Must conduct, arousing no delay,
Forever.

SOUL ON GRAVEL

Truck ruts on gravel,
fallen branches strewn among
rotted roadside trash,

fracture the architecture
of her avid attention.

She privileges
the disturbing sides of life,
doomed heartheld relics.

As though a windridden forest
of flames, she clutches time aloft.

Unsettled women
gently smooth the world around
them with their nerves lit.

In bright rooms I look away
to where the transcendent waits.

Beads of rain sliding
down a dusty window pane,
preliminary

drivebys are what life offers
fitful kings, queens, peasants, swains.

When mistakes are made,
is the committed error
from second guessing

daughters and sons or from shunning outright
beforehand mothers and fathers terrified
by male strife, predator-take-all capitalists,
and cack-tongued, anti-social democrats?

SPACE

Books worth waiting for
amidst suspect silences
are books worth writing.

Space never dies, does not burn;
never gets sick, does not age.

Wars are moments lost.
Battles are instances won.
Wars end. Wars begin.

Worlds arise here, amidst space;
disintegrate, as does sense.

I find someone's cheap
pen glinting on plush carpet
in Izmir beneath empty chairs

at the outer banks of my
attention, leaving a hall.

Days later in Thessaloniki I lose
my own expensive gold-plated pen.
The cheap one writes well,

even better than the one
now bombarding memory.

Space is never hurt,
resting upon no thing here;
changeless, has no ground.

Desire for aversion,
a version, diversion.

I move on to Crete, then
Paris, where with a view,
I've a room next to a summer

Iris stall. On Crete alone, the
lull overwhelmed me. I'll do
it all again next year,
even lose a cheap or plated pen.

TEMPORARY CLARITY

It's hard being even
Myself in my own mind
These days. She is beginning
To repeat herself, my wife,
But I pay attention because
The stories are new and recent
Experiences. She doesn't blemish
Them with embellishments: they
Stream through one another
Refreshed.

One day somehow, through
Endless associations, she
Reached into our daughter's
Desire to have a house of her
Own: the nesting instinct,
Don't you see, she revealed?

Among the very deepest of
Ambivalences and bewilderments,
Not like a disturbing new nor an old
Changing on cue, slowing a bit, but bold,
I surfaced empty-handed and unrelaxed,
Bobbing blind past the openness of
My own desires. But looking, how
Do I see, except by detecting pages
Rustling under the force of a strong wind,
Or the sound of water through the walls,
Throughout the house shutting off?

Some words baffle further conversation:
An attack of the heart? No: a heart attack.

A stroke of the heart, then? No.
A heart stroke, then?
No: A stroke. Just a stroke.
          Attack   Stroke.
Some things are merely understood.
Some things are redundant as wood.

AT TOPRAKTAN PATISSERIE

What happens in a woman's or man's heart
          in a foreign land
          is no one's affair.
What happens to their hearts
          in an alien land
          is under everyone's glare.

The heart of an ailing alien stranger
is familiar geography,
trodden territory,
excavated estuaries,
where thousands of lives have drowned
in diamond lit patisseries
among the hum of drink machines
the fragrances of custards and creams;
the constant rhythm of songs
          in the chocolate air
the whir of cash and coins,
the sashay of waitresses' loins
interrupting the sun's stare.

Where do the words come
Where do they enter
          in   from
as the radio beneath the trays of baklava
attends to the patio and the verandah?

From the earth, they say: the soil, the ground,
the land. So as night stumbles in over broken
slivers of light, invading and stumbling among
waves, particles, and dimensions between Smyrna
and Izmir; as couples strut, stroll, stroke, along
the middle of the street, down the edge of evening,
among the fleet of peanut stands, flower vendors:
aromas arise; of roasted chestnuts and fresh green
almonds, and I surmise by the time dusk reaches
the corner that they are no longer concerned with
understanding and meaning.

BLEEDING OUT

What thing is bleeding out now
That takes a presumptuous bow
Nonetheless from time to time;
Measuring the limits of our fear,
Infecting us far and wide, and near,
Challenging us to recognize kinship
Rather than breaking the sly hip
Bone now with a blessing?

I am swallowed by checkbook dyslexia,
By the inclination to walk away from
Confrontation, by the pattern of adoption
Permeating the family body, spirit, and
History.

My personal inner searches parallel
My classroom, workshop teachings.
The concrete, abstract flowing forces
Through what comforts and throttles
Me are lessons from the Moses
Heart of us, once our Ibrahim's
Brain smashes all idols.
Temptation, obsession, corruption; then
Redemption, but only after taking it in,
On the chin and dying.

VIII. IMMORTAL ARCHEAOLOGY

A HINGED-SPRUNG GATE

I like music but I go
In and out of it like
A cat slipping through
A swinging hinged gate.
It's the spring that noodles
Incongruent sound into the air.

On an overcast day,
A plane takes the sky to ground
I eye forever, sprung.

SOME

Some loving the idea so much, chin boldly
Gurning, squeeze God so hard, they can
Barely catch their breath. Sins merely
Giving them space to breathe through realmed
Revolutionary excesses of intellect, amorality,
And romanticism. We can never be They, nor
Them. Forgive me my boldness here, Oh, ThouOr,
Whether we chant Thou or Thoum to Theem,
Thoum
Art
One.

There's always some truth in presentations. However,
The full-throated embrace of optimism on this planet
Misses the point that we are now on the verge of
Destroying Gaia and not just each others' armies. The
Encouragement to look within may not be what will
Lead to solving this problem, but, rather, to get the hell
Out, off, and start over elsewhere in the galaxy.

It will not matter, though.
For the path is always toward
Home.

Trial runs. That's the feeling, and we just cannot believe it,
As if it's just our runaway imagination on a runway of its own,
This imperfect Government's version of a fascism manifesto

Tome.

BY CONTRACT

No doubt in some dark or well lit
Corner, angle, crevasse, or rupture,
All power is unjust. For there
Is where the powerless are
Victimized, even as the meek
And the naked suffer by unequal
Measure.

The darkest of our centuries, gone
And to come, recede into hymns,
Scholarship, and text books, wholly
Renarrated on holy or memorial days,
Or final exams; for victory is safer
Savored in an armchair, desk, or pew.

Why are there always bystanders
Who never seek the whites of others'
Eyes, who acquiesce toward
The increase in cavernous
Cadaverous litter?

A friend or neighbor, no longer
Potential, maimed or slaughtered,
Is too innocent or weak to comprehend,
To nurture and teach. Firepower close
Or distant stills all moral pause.

Bound by contract and existence,
Renegotiation is gnawed, governed
By impossible or improbable claws.

IN EXILIC TIME

In exilic time
     When and where
     We are alert
To constant cycles
     Of the present where
     We have been always
     One another's mother,
Empires collapse, men abdicate
On crutches and canes
To constant pasts born
Anew with the new where
We lose all sense of time.
What we do not understand
Plainly,
Clearly,
Yet
Is that there is no time,
     No time at all;
     Only space
     And motion
     And movement
Forward, backward,
In, out, through,
Where, when, men should
Never leave women behind,
Nor abandon on the run.

For every untold history,
There is an even longer one
Moaning out for a storyteller
Of aches and pains.

For every spring there, here,
There is the natural flow
Of eternal worlds with
Winters of frozen fountains
And ponds aglow.

NO MORE THAN THAT

There are people whose names I know,
And perhaps their faces also, whose
Obituaries I pass over without
A second thought, and plant not even
A clover of thought. It is only now
I begin to unbury why. It is only now
That I realize, after all these years, that
My name and face, too, will not be even
An unconscious road sign to some readers'
Casual perusal of the untimely pages of
Print and photos.

Obits as bios teach us that we are timewise
Neighbors. Nothing much more than that
Since they all read more or less the same,
Except for those in The New York Times.
And that is the point: that we are more
Or less the same, created equally; alive
Unequal.

How complete are we?
Will we evolve more
Or die as we are born?
In fact, who wants to be
More than that?

In the middle of mysteries
Of unknown histories,
How do we awake
There where
Unity and individuality
Are the same?

SPOOLING BLUE

Where and when is it
That our nature is
Actually human? Or are
We actually that: what
It is to be actually human?

In suburban or exurban brains
Lurks an
Inner city
Hillbilly
Reservation
Barrio
Predator.

At the center of the universe,
Of its own presence, apparently,
Finite dust has emerged from
The hand of infinity.

Recently,
As I slept sprawled on
The sofa, spooling blue
Across my screen was
The next truth serum
Distraction shimmering
Forward: a video or document
Accessing our constant
Attention of one of many
Purveyors sharing daily reports
On the nations.

There is this screenlit piety
Among us of spiteful shruggers,
News men and women in halfway
Offices, who lean in toward one
Another to sip spit from the fountain
Of one another's mouth.

From their mouths to our ears,
They treat us as their eager gods.

All of a sudden, lightning from
The night air outside lit up my room.
Then the explosion next: first light
Then thunder, crashing into
My sleep and home. This thunder
Storm punctuated my heart
Before my heart conjured up groans
And sentences for life.
The back and forth flow
Of dimensions and infinity
That we choose to enter to
Spend time with our dim
And lurid demons
And angels in fear, honor,
And interest, and be
Neither a ruin nor an anomaly
Forever, in a self-loving society,
Frames our constant enflamed dreams
Of planes bodyslamming into
Skyscrapers penetrating the
Air, of brains freefloating into
The air to save their bones, at least.

In the dreaming, gleeful,
Deranged, weakened eyes will
Spot dust everywhere in any
Angle of sunlight. What
Of the future itself, does it
Bring something to us or
Hold something for us until
We arrive there, unburdened,
Burdened and interested?

GRIEF UNDER LIGHT

Hypatia often wondered,
        Imagined even,
What he would be like,
        And decided however
That curiosity is sweeter
        Than knowledge
Braced and hilted
        By dark fidelity,
And so vowed to devour
Only under light
And be devoured by
        The quest of the unfamiliar,
The unreliable,
        The enduring,
The assured and unpredictable.
Thus in grief
        She often wondered
And therefore under light
        Often abandoned belief.

A LEGEND IN HIS OWN MIND

I'm trying, Rachel, I'm trying,
He said, slipping away, satchel
In hand

Before she could retort and rebuke
Him with, Yes, you are, you really
Are!

And hoped she hadn't pretended
That fluke in language, that
Double entendre that he hadn't
Actually intended.

It's like thumbtacking on your office
Door the note Out To Lunch!
And having noonday co-worker
Passers-by snicker, Yes, he truly
Is, isn't he?, corroborating office
Lore.

Self-erasure and a contrary world's
Futility dog his heels over the long
Slog of war recounted in the papers
Daily. He saddens deeply over swirls
Of tyranny from the soil of this land
Of words fired from a civil war
Between ideology and honor,
Foreign occupation and loyalty; and
Ever so deeply over images of warriors'
Desecrated bodies tagged and stacked
And left as oddities, like dead bees,
Moths, and flies shrouded in dust
On the back shelves of deserted libraries,
Coffeehouses, hospitals, bookstores, or
In the crevices of civic lobbies and halls.

Cycles open and close: Hurricanes,
Earthquakes and typhoons
Ravage the earth.

Stay in touch!, friends hurrying off amused
In opposite directions often shouted at
His back.

I'm certainly touched if I do, he often mused.
Red friends, black friends, brown friends, yellow friends, white
friends,
      —Fear!
Rich friends, poor friends, fat friends, skinny friends, dull friends
       —Yawn!
Creeping friends, sleeping friends, leaking friends, moping friends
       —Flee!

Should he proof that student's thesis
Or this student's book manuscript?
Should he crack open that book
Newly arrived in the mail? Or
Will he simply, quietly, go to pieces?

Should he tramp outside to fill bird
Feeders? Should he slip into his white
Boots to plant new irises around the pond?
Or crawl back into bed until another dawn?

Once outside, should he chop away at
That broken branch or sprinkle
More coyote urine granules around
The garden bark to warn off amber-eyed
Raccoons slinking in the dark?
Should he daydream longer here
At the kitchen window? Or shuffle
Across this huge family room
To his rocking chair?

Should he
Brew another cup of tea?

Wake me when you're up,
The note taped to the kitchen
Cabinet reads.

I've been trying for years, he thought.

HOUSE BIRTH

Above her head
A portrait hung,
Its eyes of things to come, a hum
Of silence, a word worthy
And dumb.

Upon the wall her visage
Of three years looked out
Across the rooms beyond
Her pregnant bed, beyond
Her widened sheets, beyond
The opposite walls of all
Her rooms of carpets, pearl,
And wood.

Beyond the sound of her
Husband who stood beyond
The dew, beside the medical
Crew who chortled forth
A child's initial poise
Among so new, so much old,
Applause.

THE GATEFOLD CELEBRATIONS

There is a last song
That boredom's sea will shape,
The last wave that slips
The net from thought,
That puts the fishermen to boat,
The wind to rake the surface of the lost.
There are sways and swirls and swells
Of the sea, stretches of seasong
Soothing the science of dreams and reason.
A song to dampen the burden of the shipbearing season
Where war has been no vacation,
No bikini campaign, nor struts across the sand.

Whisper to the bird uncataloged by shelves,
Whose bottommurky sweep
Across our face
Pauses, a comma in the sky,
Grasping the air where
Whirls of winds loom,
While sailors ravel aside
Their mothers' lace and womb.

Bury our hands beyond maimed doors,
Old hands, dead hands; bury our knees
At the river's unflowing, color our eyes
In green and blood, shroud our mouths
In wind and mud. We are whispers
Of the warriors' lonegoing.

I bear no tendency of light nor sound,
Nor stammer my throat on the ground.
Seems to be a soft passage ahead,
A corridor of gleams,
The way concentration disperses,
Rapids swirling in my dreams.

Losers bury conquerors at night,
Turning out invasions in their sleep,

But we?
But we light a corner of our tent
Where battle maps may keep
The land our gain and innocent.

These moments of song
Preventing refusal, songs humming
Their windmindful woods around our sighs,
Propel us along the path of error,
Pulsate us from rock to rock,
Swinging and squeaking our fears now nearer,
Clanging shut, hinging in an inert gate of cells,
The clamor of seaweed, the calm of watermuffled bells.

The suns are ascending at our left,
Splaying their heat into the breeze,
The earth caressed seems to move,
A flow upon foundations,
A heave beneath the grass,
A wind avenue of trees.

TURNTAKING

Today's newspapers misspelled another tale:
Of a suicide dying by an old couple's selves,
Whose feeling knowledge of pleasure had
Remade itself implicit among the shelves
Of books and candlefire dust.

Nothing evolves like the living
As the eternal precision and location
Of the invisible, carnal world
Where the cosmic rootlessness of the new
Infers its form from the lateral, faithful clue.

Where they met was a handsome day,
Distant and oncoming, and the beauty
Of the moments could not abandon its femininity.
He, what must he be
But try to be the sun, skincomprehending,
Javelining along thought and beyond,
Closing in, spermglinting.
Death is the shift of fringes,
A lambent sigh of explorations.

MAKEDA'S KINSHIPS

1

Out of me the grief,
Love of place and residence,
The patience of rock and tin.
The battle tank, shopping cart,
Stagecoach and pram: useful kin.

2

Whenever over centuries I have
Looked at a map, my blood boils
Up in grief, in loneliness. While
Ethiopia, Gao, Yugoslavia bled,
Storytellers always visited us.

3

In unbearable
Whispered conversations
She reveals every detail
In intimate diaries
Secrets of strangers like me.

4

With the remotest
Accuracy, how often
Must he remember
To beg soulfelt forgiveness,
To love the swollen, bloated child?

5

My mind strolls at night
Collecting conversations,
Memorializing debts.
My soul owes to dead persons
Lost ideas, shriveled regrets.

6

From the other side,
Will one child remember me?

Who aborted whom?
Foot blooming from her forehead.
Protracted mind darkwater clear.

7

To the rose how fresh
Are we who pleasures anew?
Whose pleasing fragrance
Unnameable leans with thorns
Awakened, awakening hush?

8

An aborted child
Occupies her brain's cold core,
A remembered child,
A pleasing fragrance unnamed,
To the rose how fresh are we?

9

A sharper gander's quill,
Never challenged, the male norm,
Bedeviled erect,
Creates the Nation's woman,
The mute, gendered citizen.

10

Arabs dragged Europe
From the dark, aging still, as
Sacajawea
And York cultivated Clark's
Notebook curiosity.

11

Fueled by opposite,
Mockery and sympathy,
I realize truth
Immersed in the expressions
Of your self-serving being.

12

Where desert truths bloom,
Rocky soil predominates.
I ache to harvest
Solely with but voice and body
Hymns beneath the desert floor.

13

On mountaintops, trees
Hug the slopes like bushy
Veins calculating risks.
In winter avalanches
Snow leopards inflame the air.

14

The budded beauty
Of insults crested her lips
Cancerous with dying words.
They leaned to her graveyard
Breath, her rabbi, priest, and imam
Blessing her rage.

A SOLDIER'S DEATH

> But was it not the death of a hero?
> Here and there are the tanks and incense
> Pacings of our past, the shipcrowned harbors,
> Fishfossiled headlands, mushroombeckoned tombs,
> All the traded ruins in quiet museums,
> And ghostly guesses inveigling for
> The tarpaulin of monument
> And hornblaring certainty.

The mountain had lifted   the jeep from its footing,
The vehicle humped   the road's rises;
The width of noon   cornered the clouds
At his brow; he   met the intake
Of day and   future nights
With eyes vasting   across the lake.
He motored through   woods khaki with the past,
Blue with the lake's   whispered sunning exploding,
Along the beige   wisdom of the bridge,
To where prospects in   his brain imploded:
Disembodied in   bullets of shrewed
Sighs, his last revisioning   across his view
       Closing.

> But who will ascend a park bench
> To speak of the years? Who will do
> This living again? Old prophets
> Are aged mirages gone from the
> Stump platforms, but always a peg
> Or two are left in the sawdust while
> Men remove like men of a carnival.

IN A BRILLIANTLY LIT ROOM

It is difficult to linger
In a brilliantly lit room

From whose audiencewalled faces
You have stolen animation

With your gesticulated hypotheses
Or with your gestured testaments.

Professor or witness, lecturer or defendant:
One of Earth's greenish consultants:

The solution is in the dissolution of the wall,
In seeing cracked lines form

Up and over the room's solidarity
Like late winter bare branches,

Just before green truth, where squirrels
Dart before the sky's bluecemented

Sun rising.

PRAYER

There are miniatures
Like this moment now
When we realize tomorrow
Won't ejaculate any more of
Easy ecstasies than today's
Inverted creation, when we hold
Our room to be no neighbor
Of momentous openings of mood
Over smiles, nor of serviceable victories.

Some blindness during a restful
Moment will claw a nimble stare,
Gasp in the corner of our room's witness,
Scorch the walls of our insight
With furnacing breath of prayer,
Prickle the close heat of the hut,
The silence of determined crossed knees,
With needling tenderness.

But we are not lost in
This awkwardness, only hurt somewhat.
Help us.

Help us resurrect above oblivious, involuntary fear.
Help us rediscover.
Help us sift the mystery of human wickedness
                    That we may cohere.

Help time and the cities
Undo us, dissuade us to a planet of abilities.

THE IMMORTALISTS

When we were youth, beamed and hummed among spacious strings,
When days in rain migrated in sunbursts to our bodies,
The universe revolving on a booked memory
Needed no passengers in ships to architect its studs.
Sleek machines of our imagination unithrust
Time, bough, chime and space. This was the ignition of our
Race, the cannonmetal goblet of our ancient quaff.

Perhaps, however, however distant first days are,
The slow pour in a rainless universe, where we have
Forever, marks our skin, and we, mummed for comfort
At our innerstory cellroom windows, clutch up our
Sheet for more warmth. The dance of transubstantiation
Perfects the interrogating presence of cold slate
In moondust adrift in fidgeting hieroglyphics.

The end of the world is not, the warmgladdened, grainy hymn
Of Earth's first brutalist limb sicklethumps the flirting plot.

IX. LISTENING IN

WAR AND PEACE

We want to be
Sent packing from wars unending
At the accurate seeing-eye hour

Home edged toward the mud-sliding precipice
Beckons our wind-shriveled, blood-shot senses
Soothes our bullet-riddled-ridden sleep
Receives our cavernous-cadaverous awakening

Peace is a flock of fed-up de-feathered pink-eyed meadow birds
Feeding on unpeeled blood oranges from our cankered mouths

War is a field of dreams of screaming, shrieking scarecrow carrion
Becoming sloven, tongue-tied-tired speeches

We need you
Where belief-free language and faithful-situations become us

Freedom breaking free
Chronicles our punch-drunk senses
Disciplines our silence-chosen weapons
Honors our enemy-turned allies

Peace is an outerspace hospital of newborn reborns
Nursed after dying and resurrection

War is an unearthed monitoring architecture
Glimpsing deceasing de-privileged government

PERSONALITY OUT ON A LIMB

Today is Friday and I am not a terrorist.
It is the first of three Sabbaths. I workout
At the uptown gym and prepare pomegranate
Pancakes with clementines and honey by
Midafternoon for my family, to remember
Once again our personal relationship with
The universe, to life. How like a drop of dew
That dines on a flash of lightning, a shadow,
A bubble, a phantasm, a dream separateness is,
        As the Buddha reminds us.

We never need to be taught but only reminded,
        For we know already, and forget,
        The soul of our souls at rest.

Across the years, at least three teachers
Censured me for inattentiveness. They
Misunderstood the nature of a rich interior
Life, mistook the hood before my face, did not,
Could not, enter the whispered darkened wood
Of well-lit images, of well-tuned voices. They
Hung me from the crosses of their imagination.

They did not look and could not see.
        They did not hear and could not listen.

Today, every day, he sat a bit here on the curb of any sidewalk
That ran along any bridge; sometimes on the west side,
Sometimes on the other side; always with his back to the
Sun. He wanted others to see him every day of their lives as they
Have wondered about the disheveled, dishelmed gait of a certain
Roadside tramp, hobo, who mumbled and never panhandled:
"Where did that old Black guy go to? Who was he anyway?
All he ever did was just sit there, staring off to the other side
Of the bridge. It's a wonder the old rat never got struck by a
Truck, sitting so close to the open road like that."
        He has disappeared, perhaps into hospice
        Or an asylum, and I will remind them of
        Missing him.

Today is Saturday and I am not a terrorist.
The soul of my soul, always a restless censer,
A vengeful censor.

It is the Sabbath.
When I write, do I express the soul of more than me,
Of more than what meets the eye; the soul of streets,
Neighborhoods, authentic houses; a family, a people?
Whose humanity do my words enfold, embrace in timbres
Blunt and bold, silver and cold, gold and hot?

Does the unseen warfare of my spirit have its own plot
Insinuated in my brain stem? How often is my personality
Out on a limb, perched above the Earth crevassing closer,
Grinding shut?

Today is Sunday. It is the Sabbath. I am not a terrorist.
Is it heavy rain that makes New Orleans quiet, niagaraing
Over balcony ledges onto banquets, banquettes and gutters?
Or is it the buildings, the dwellings themselves, that give
Our showers this illumination of pillared blessings
And romantic baptisms?

I will now drive once more across town past stores,
Bookshops, coffeehouses, bars, bistros, bodegas, malls,
Making my way toward the Lake to the north halls;
But heavy traffic first, then the wooded country roads
And wooded silences of rabbits and squirrels underbrush;
Of an occasional hawk, egret, or young buck, in the rush
Of evening folding out over oaks, azaleas, and magnolias,
Revealing the moon and the ravens at rest; the vultures
Unseen till
Morning, loping down
Over road kill.

PHANTOM'S AUTUMNAL FANTASY

Will I be the first to die?

Whose shudder touched me, there
At my right shoulder?
Show yourself. Come
Unto me. Teach me.
Give me intuition,
Visions; fortitude and
Strength: years upon
Years to make her proud,
My shy eyes-averted bride.
        We often read about a spouse
        Dying, whose mate sooner or
        Later without skyopening reasons
            Comes upon another,
        A new friend, or a truer mate
        For the first time. They marry
        Or shack up for no reason
        Or rhyme. Can we live now with
        That eventuality, that horror,
        To be replaced, to have stepped
        Aside into death and then
        To be put aside without a divorce,
        With such assured annulment?

        Will she then imagine she's
        Never been happier when her toes
        Curl, or her aging calves charlie-horse cramp,
        In pained ecstasy, and she whispers lies to him
        She's so sorry they had not met
        Earlier? What does that mean?
        That finding him she would have
        Left me or that she now wished
        Her young self had never been
        Disrupted by my sudden surge?
        Why would she cull forth such
        A cruel, sad plea, except that
        Her guile imagines him as me?

Am I already an aging apparition
Appendix?
Will I die first?
Will I die first?

I cannot imagine being the second to flow away, clutching
Immemorial time to fall upon someone
More adorable than she who left: My forever
Companion sidekick whom I never could have hidden away in my
Fedora? What nagging, angel-demonic thoughts
Are these holding on to my spouse so near, who will
Always touch me there at my shoulders?

DEVOUR MY BREATHING

Time and times grow so far below
The sheen of noticed events that
We only suspect perturbations
That we might learn to study but
Never expect to see as we steal
Glances through our notes and
Dreams of so many particles
Waved and woven living below
Time, outside of space, where
Gravity never comes to rest among
The flow and float of so much matter
Evolving out.

I recall the day no different from this
Lean day of every August in Thessaloniki
When the gunmetal blue of the Aegean
Snarls and snuffles toward the curb
Of the seawall below the sidewalk, where
The summer haze of mist suggests secrets
Hissed by the scintillating breathing of
The sea among the deeper, darkening breaths
Below.

Life here above the seawall satisfies its own
Linear instincts by its ability to pull and
Push, slaughter and maim. Below the line
Of sight and experience floats the scrum
Of beauty. Horizons sting our eyes, grow restless:
Horizons of buried limbs and thighs, recession lines,
Traffic light lines, criminal court lines, tuition lines,
Toilet lines at opera houses.

Which way one faces is significant. I imagine
God looking over at Darwin (Some might say
Looking down), thinking, "There is my son
Charles, studying his brethren of other
Forms, documenting that matter moves itself
And creates new species." The only central

Law is the law of the struggle for existence
That our and His works may interpret our
And His words.

We never learn what heaven has emanated
And matter wrought until we look around
In the world, in all the worlds; in the universe,
In all the universes. So voyage. Go out to
Come into ourselves again.

I sniff at my metaphors as much as I like,
Nibble at the edges. You may not scorn my
Long pauses nor my shortness of breath.
Devour my breathing or in and out of your
Own brain take a hike.

What do we know? What don't we know? Stem
Memory of bees and birds push each generation
Home again. The blood of Phrygians still hems
The borders of Asia Minor and Achaea as the
Hybrid bodies of Kurds, Armenians, Greeks,
Nubians and Turks.

Though here below in our yards of fenced-in
Breathlessness where revenge gnaws against
Forgiving, betrayal preens naked before the hand
Of trust, measures the messiness of life against
The nagging, calculating mosquito fact of unseen
Reality and mystery.

Scan the depths of the human brain for its
Desolations, hesitations, lunges, silences.
Choose the wayfaring darkened forests
Of memory and notice there has been no
Change in the tangled, entwined blood
Rivulets of each cell's snuggled webbing
From and toward oneness.

I want to know how determined and free
The universe is and am content to start

With this world first and move on to bleed
Among other worlds next, from each to
Each, and from universe to universe, to
Know their wars, as my ashes rise to mingle
With carbon gases and amino acids exploding
From the fungi of their stars.

Study the shape and finitude of the universe
We get to frame within our touch, gaze, or
Flight.

Study how the hidden infinite structures of
Random ordered chaos in the universe behave
As our patient heart glimpses curved beauty
Just within reach with intuition and sousreal
Numbers' insight.

Stars and galaxies, light, time, and gravity are
The tattoos on our skin, the jewels in our hair.

The hidden balance of mischievous universes
Will teach us how truly free is the fare.

Step off.

PHOTOS FROM RIALTO BEACH

I've noticed about myself over the years
The first thing I look for in parent-forwarded
Photos of newborns among us is a sense of
Presence in the face. This kid I am now
Studying among twelve true new shots, as
The lens catches him commemoratively
In the universe, is his being fully present
In all of his captured moments. He has a
Sense of curiosity already there.

I especially like the subtle photo here,
With the father's gentle presence
And support graciously invisible at the
Edge as his child at the center satisfies
Curiosity, leaning out without tremor
From his father's tethered grasp a clutch
Of knuckles and fingertips, to press
            The solemnity of a
            Starfish creviced
            By waves against
            An idle rock
            Seabalanced.

AGONISTIE TOWARD CHEF MENTEUR

Sometimes I am sensitive to light and sound
And on occasion will forget simple dependence
On myself or others, and will become eyefatigued
Or distracted. Other times I am fully aware and
Vigilant, stilled by a bright-eyed intelligence of
Those in the room or at the table. Sometimes we
Learn from hurt choking on the chew of others.

I should not say to you, Here I am, a body.
Rather: here I am, in a body. Here in bodies
We gather. But what are we the reverse of,
The opposite of, the alternative to? What
Gods or idols do we misconstrue? Are we
Visitors who have lost track, time, and space?
Or are we questions withdrawing within to
Seek immortal responses?

The question is its own response.

I know syllables, I know words. Never
Living, never lifeless, always alive.
Persistent stories, though foolish
Since they are not unique, embody
Language and wisdom, never lies.

He disturbed me toward no beginning. It
Was all an end. I sloshed as far away from
Him as I could escape toward Chef Menteur and
Arabi through swamps, slouching through
Slush at four miles an hour. I stopped for a map
And duct tape for my soiled new Pumas that
Were crumbling apart in the muck under my
Anger. Just before sunset, in Metairie I bought
Bottles of water and a rucksack. Soon, I covered
      Forty miles with forty pounds
      Upon My grandfatherladened back.

I slaked my sorrow by hacking the malehag
To pieces in my mind as I trudged across
The swamps. There in horror he had lain,
     Chafing his pious hands,
     Beating and smoothing
     His bed linen draped
Across his chest. He deleted my story with
A new tale I had never heard tell. On his
Drunken sick bed, not quite dead, he dismantled
My longed for identity. His thick hidden to others
Hatred of me from my birth to now wisped from
His drugged stupor across his breast. Some part
Of him secreted deep within his bowels knew what
Sickened lost family criminality he was perfecting.

Was this confession or retribution I was to suckle?

Did he bless me with truth or curse me with a lie?
Whose child am I? Am I white or black? Native or
Adopted at the border?

For the first time in my life, conflicted, I felt
I had to tame myself to him, this dagger of a
Spirit whom I once loved before. Now a sudden
Stranger, he appeared beneath those sheets
Wrinkled fiercely by kicking feet.

Who was this Chalmette male sinking before me,
This blustering, spitting, croaking Thing? This thing in hate?

This *That*!

Is spoken, spat hatred a revelation that is supposed
To guide us out of our ego toward full, clear knowledge
Of self, of the hidden love in a hater flailing, coughing
Sputtered words creating us anew? A love threaded in hatred
Cleaves.

Has a male sociopathic heaven been plotting false dreams and desires
In my brain? Through the swamps, falling, stumbling

Away from him, I wept, scouring my running nose
Across my sleeves.

The world is mad.
Where in which heaven surveils
My generation's god?

I never hitch rides, but there he was, a young, new
Thing, offering me a ride to anywhere up ahead
In a deep blue Mustang.

For levity, I poked the air with my hitchhiker's thumb,
Then both nailencrusted thumbs. We both laughed.
He had spotted me up the road slipping the edge of the
Mudsucking swamp, waiting until I neared a clearing
Of two roads merging. Slowing up, he laid
Back by an impulse to aid. I am aware of angels
And demons descending in a time of fits and crises.
I, still a virgin, my twin Agonistes
In uniform away in Afghanistan, I climb
Aboard anyway.

If ever I allowed myself to think about all that
Others have accomplished and I hardly nothing,
I would throw up constantly in the night and
Thump my emptying heart in misery for never
Getting anything exactly, or even slightly, right.
                    Now,
Migraine arrows of fear, desire, memory, mystery
Jerked, not slipped elegantly from my quiver,
flick, not snap, from the bow of memory, quibbling
            Off against the light.

PIETY MAIMED

We do not want you to tell us about joy.
We want you to create joy. We want you
To be music to us, not like newspapers.
Dislike reigns worldwide, however.
Disgruntled piety shapeshifts devotion
Into hatred. Reverence and Adoration
Step back out of sight in shame.

Muslims glorify 99 Names of the Divine's
Attributes. Jews worship the One Alone, who,
Never needing to create Himself, released forth
9 Emanations of the Divine Self as both hosts
And guests in the Universe. Christians worship
3 Persons of the Godhead whom they glorify
As One; yet lust to be the only ones for the One
          Only infant slumbering snug
          In the crib of their grasp.

Sloth, willful ignorance, and stupidity
Have ever been their daily subtle duress.
Yet all their life of devotion and mutuality
Will remain for us as thin, crustless finger
Sandwiches and hibiscus punch. When facing
One another over lunch, every chat among
Their 33,000 denominations, even the nons,
As centurion touchless lovers or touched
Enemy heretics, breathe oblique conversations
On their backs,
On heir sides,
Or side by side.
          99, 9, 3 = 111 = 3 in image and likeness.
          Attributes, Emanations, Persons. Where
          Can there be error in such beauty? What
          Meek Elegance is it that human piety
          Cannot see in three Sabbaths at rest
          Once a week?

EL JESÚS

Imagining history, we come undone
       Like afterbirth.
They deny sixteenth-century Africans
Boosted Britain's engine of superiority,
The Industrial Revolution, that all of blighted
       Europe lustily ignited?
       The narrative is not poetic.

The trade in nations birthed from Africa's soil rose
Up slave-trading seaport towns of Bristol, Liverpool,
Nantes, Bordeaux, and Seville. They shall forget
Their source of the first mining and minting origin
Of the seventeenth-century Dutch gold coin,
Of the United Kingdom's guineas. Shall we forgive,
Forget and not suggest, nor teach, Jemaimah's
Intention that Africanus, her son, descend enslaved
Upon the Americas, Britain, and Europe to sootheshape
The West and Africa into a body of one some century
To come? From the narrative evolves a sacred revelation.

       Did fifteen million have to die en route, we gasp?
       The Indigenous New World nations could not
       Withstand European diseases, nor survive
           Africa's mines,
           America's plantations.
Hardy West turned toward hardier, disciplined Africa
For Africa's nations. John Hawkins, England's first slaver,
Kidnapping four hundred in Guinea in 1562, traded
       Them in the West Indies for Elizabethan
           Pearls, ginger,
           Sugar, and hides.
       He sold stolen Africans to the Spanish
       In America. Elizabeth I rewarded his
       Success with seaworthy *El Jesús*, a sailing
       Ship. Soon she pronounced him a knight.

       As his noble coat of arms, Hawkins chose
       A buttnaked African in chains: A bound

African for the trade he pioneered
For the Empire, and for all of Europe.
            So much for so little,
            Surely we die
            More than once
            Birth after birth.
To get it never right. Perhaps.

VISIONS REMOTE AND TIGHT

There are days when I so hunger
For the western and eastern Aegean
Food chain that I can understand
How life can be difficult for so many
Down on this remote planet in its
Revolve and rotate in remote space
          And near-time.

How might we stroll or even march into
An Edenic wilderness where we may reveal
To Self hidden delayed urges to face splendid
Mysteries of our deepest inner caves and lairs?

What difference does what any of us do
Make when debates become scuffles and
Scuffles turn into war? Is war meant
          To save the planet?

What of war with the planet? The Mississippi,
Curled along the Louisiana Purchase
For centuries, continues to shrug and push
Against its coasts, brimming the Atchafalaya,
New Orleans, and Baton Rouge; Morgan City
Ruined. Where tornado and hurricane seasons
Rage in earnest this year, Joplin lies splintered.
          Ruined.

Is it my thin age now that corners me against these
Tight visions? Whatever became of the awed child
Who, innocent every hurricane season, would yell
From the front door's latched screen, "Mom, Look!
Come see! See, the winds are twisting an' bending
The trees, an' rattling the fence an' gate! Come see,
Ma! Ma!"

Guilt askance has putrified, perfumed mankind forever. It matters
Little that we are distracted by complexity or fear;
Both emerging from caution of others. Soon radios,

Computers, and screens of every sort embracing news
In parallel surrounds will leer through the centuries.

> Storm candles will no longer brighten
> A mere flicker of memory.

THREE HEAVY DOORS

All around me friends have been dying
Unnatural deaths, their bodies decaying
From inside out. At first, when parents
Of friends died, I thought it natural, for
It was their time. But it is not now time
For the light around the brain of friends
To dim, fade, recede, turn dark, and turn
                    Off.
I turn aside from natural and unnatural
Deaths. May we turn away inner wars?

Socialist Stalin slew billions of his own
To hew a path for those coming afterwards
So the newly born anew may be embraced
Under the tent off communism. But what
Slays my friends this century but hybrid
Modified nourishment produced by America's
Lust for capital, produced by ignorant
Narcissists' piety and prayer for Armageddon.

            Today the religious are psychopathic.
            Sometimes I am overwhelmed
            By the traffic of trivia
            Crisscrossing America's cortex.

            The impurity of war is its mere
            Unexpected existence, its
            Unimagined execution:
            Messiness in politics
            Leading to it,
            Following it,
            Nursing
            Its presumed, presumptuous
                        End.

HELEN

Helen. Who has ever deeply thought
Of Helen? Troy's Helen, be that as it will.
Given what our women and men have submitted
Their spirits to in Europe, Vietnam, Somalia,
Benin, Afghanistan, Iraq, she seems today like
An insignificant lover blinged by beauty, a sheen
Of inadvertent skin, a voluptuous innocence
Who stumbled upon our stages from an antique
Poem about battle-ready, half dressed, accurate
And inaccurate mythic men and women to emulate.
           Was it their
         Gods and Achaean Heroes
         Who sent us on to wars
        Across ages of sages?
              Did Achilles's
              Myrmidons
              Ever weep
              For her
Or have at forlorn Paris only out of male loyalty
To choked sighs and smeared wedding vows?
Are they today why so many lean into erotica Attica?

YOUR MOTHER'S FUNERAL

How much more invisible
        Must I be
In a room where all faces
Are attentive as poppies
        On stems
Before you remember
To greet and commend me
As you have the others,
Believers, agnostics, atheists,
Unbelievers, polytheists,
        Before Him
Below His Altar?

Is my face not worthy of a name?
Or is it that I have the gift
Of fading into the frame?

I, too, was a friend to you,
Your family, or so I thought,
And to your mother who lay
In state, by Death bought.

But here sprawl sorrow, hurt,
And anger; of fraternal triplets
In tears on the funeral floor.

    Hidden
Beneath my pew, once again,
My unvoiced blank face, unbidden,
    Shouts.

WATCHFUL ARCHIVE

Going over my head,
          Commandeering the moment
          Against my will and wishes,
Nature pulled me into her
Watchful archive as I awakened
          Against the snorting bull
          Dozing deeper and deeper
Into the earth to make room
For more apartment buildings
          Where town farmers will no
          Longer plot ground to grow
Fresh vegetables from the soil.

The bulldozer for months now
          Punctuates morning, afternoon,
          And evening prayer; the all
Night vigil in our brain. We can
No longer sense the difference
          Between the echo and the source;
          Of pounding metal raping the earth
In the indiscrete summer heat or rain.

Everywhere I turn, new apartments
          Spiral like bone spurs along
          The spine of the hills above
Their valleys, our nearby alleys,
And the sea on the other side.
          But for their glistening new false
          Wood, their brittle steel beams,
The unfinished structures
Round about might be
          Mistaken for blighted,
          Bombed-out shelters.
The earlier buildings
Here and there adorning
          Izmir in yellows will
          Turn the page for us.
Soon the olive groves,

The mulberry trees,
     The apple orchards, fields
     Of poppies, will shimmer
Into swimming pools
And parking lots and
     I will miss the vigilant
     Crow of the farmers'
Roosters kept up all night
By the workmen's camp light.

Every machine a war machine,
Even the borders of lamps at night.

IN TIME IN ASIA MINOR

In time, all veils fall away.
I have been stuck in moments
Like this before, in the middle
Of summer heat, with no means
To wander off on my own; not even
On my own two feet; a house guest,
Like the sacrificial goat tethered
In the shade of a tree, with anywhere
And nowhere to stalk off to, as if
My body or the world were running
Out of spectrum.

'From dust to dust', as 'From day
To day', takes on real, new meaning
Whenever I notice dust motes swirling
In my dining room along the fall of sun
Lighting its way through the blind slats
Of my window. Dust is everywhere, dust
Day after dust day, from human skin,
From the soles of feet, cast off clothes.

The city's generations one from the other
Differ so greatly over the last decades.

Above where I sunbathe on my fourth
Floor balcony, at this hour the sun now
Hangs parched against walls of the city.
Though I long for comforting, cinched
Cloth and cloak in my own quiet neighborhood
Habous, Ashram, Skete, or Shul, on my own two
Feet I slip in and out of a visitor's understanding
And a tourist's knot.

An aimless bee motors the banana breath rim
Of my rum glass. I feel I have already died
From too much Abrahamic hospitality.

A WORLD WITHOUT CANVAS

Can we imagine   a world without
a canvas of words   that against
their will   will not twist
against meaning;   a universe of no
discernible border,   no boundaries;
of simultaneous   open flow
in all   directions?

Under the hood
of my head lies
my brain's private   experiences
out of awareness,   where half
of me is others at rest.

What part of us
was never
born and cannot die?

What part of me
tumbling out of and away
from my frame
in and out of season
is at war

with every alive   and dead Maple leaf,
with every   summer cottonmouth
seeking warmth   lurking through
webbed firewood   stacked to the rafters

In back of the carport?   Should I leave a question
undone, bejeweled   with silence, or part
and lean the sighs   of its angles

against
quantum nothingness'
opening spaces?

ONE AWFUL THING AFTER ANOTHER

A young personal caretaker submitted false timesheets
Attesting that she had provided to patients services
Of bathings, groomings, cooking, and cleaning.
            She will go to prison on ten counts of fraud.

A young Alabama man burglarized eight upscale suburban
Homes south of Military Road in Turtle Creek and French Branch.
            He will go to jail.

A young man booted his best friend to death as they argued
Over the meaning of vicious visionary Biblical passages.
            He will go to prison.
On Monday, in Shawnee, Oklahoma, his life companion will
Be buried in tribal clothing by his aunt who had raised
            And nurtured him.

During the night, on his Gentilly front porch, the breath of a 99
Year old oyster shucker was squeezed from his lungs by someone
yet unknown. He had cooked meals for regiments in Okinawa
            And Marseille in WW1.

On some days thirty, or on other days sixty, obituaries I glance
Over, gaze at, or read; of folks who die natural deaths, as we
Say. Or from the usual untimely modern ailments: cancer, diabetes,
Pneumonia, heart disease, lupus, leukemia, embolism, accidents.
Or from the occasional unreported mysterious dying from day
By day anxiety-ridden drumming on the brain of interior
Quibbles, replayed arguments, angry dialogues, shouts, and screams.

Or from medical complications, staph infections, new market
Medications, environmental pollutants, suicide, heartbreak.
                        Can we ever name these boundaries
                        More accurately?

X. ILLUMINATION
AND BLINDING

CORNERED

She is known for
A handful of novels,
A handbagful of poems,
A purseful of essays
Yet here she sits,
In a French Quarter hall,
Receiving nothing,
Crouched against the south
Back wall behind a room full
Of luncheon friends and guests
Of celebrants receiving awards
Of recognition for a smatterful
Of accomplishments.
Her hair roots
Whitened imperceptibly more
In Creole resentment. Thinking
Herself clever
She swore
And promised herself never
To create another piece of work
Until Louisiana learned to share
Her with the nation, with people
Who read and attend,
Who attend and read.
Lost among the seats,
"I will be your Never-Whore!" her
Teeth hiss in uterine rage.
"What was that?" a neighbor asks,
Distracted, engaged. "Navajo. I am
Thinking about writing about the Navajo
Next." She whispers, averted eyes ablaze.
As if talking to no one.
Uneasy in her chair,
She has an urge to leave. Her bowels flare.
Actually, this conversation never took place.
It went off only in her head. She is a writer
After all, and envy often narrates its path
In our Southern brain.

Her bowels in stress pushed her deeper
          Into her cushioned pain.
She sees herself getting older in her students'
Eyes. She no longer knows what they do not know
And know, nor what they want to know. Why are they
Even here, she wonders constantly? Have I nothing
To offer but quizzical stares to their silence? What
She suspects to be true is that their former school
Teachers, like their parents, are lost among scrotum
               Patriarchy.
Boys, who do not want to attend university, register
Anyway to major in whatever their fathers recommend.
Girls, their babies left with grandmother during registration
Week, choose to study sociology, psychology, or education.
               Never
Read to as babies by a working household, they have little interest
In literature. Half of these bristling youth are medicated, as elementary
Teachers insisted should be so so long ago. Managed and managing,
          Their parents are drugged, and abandoning;
               Their babies, like poems
                  Dark and light,
                  Damaged.

HIGH HOLY DAYS

I am empty on this Pesach, Pascha weekend.
No matter how much unbelievable despair
I grind out to purchase unthinkable unseen
Mid-life rabbinical or ecclesiastical shifts
In understanding, forgiveness, and pardon,
The only emolument entering the rooms of
Every cell of my limbs is the morning smell
Of French coffee, Vietnamese afternoon tea,
Cold German evening white wine. I cannot
Even prophesy a good, fine future by creating
It myself. No caffeine, rosehip, or tannin will
Help. No Simon Magus I.

Nor do I want to be. I am not that calculating.
What I would like to believe is that heaven
Believes in me, even as I falter, or stand forth
In courage, as atheists would say. Out of nowhere,
So it still seems, emerging divine order and human
Purpose, glinting, coaxing, dismantling, settling
In. Life hands out and holds out more choices.
With the rains come growth; with growth,
Overgrowth and new withering. With discoveries
Come stars, planets and moons; eruptions,
Explosions, and settling in anew. What changes
Is the sentient being, and the word human in
Different grunts, languages, and misplaced
                    Or lost throats.

WIDOWER'S LAMENT

It is a god who does not live
          Who explains.
Your aerial voices are under wind
          And plain
As streams in a backwood,
Not a small, smooth chip
          Of a good
Waterdrop underside a floating leaf.

And they are asleep now,
          Those two,
Man and woman by the door,
By the gate of where they are not,
Of where they have not been:
          They die their lives
          In the hood of their youth.

I sit here now in their backroom,
          Taking my memory apart
With a photo album that ought to put
It together again, but does not;
          A parlor maid friend
Volunteering to stack the dishes and the bones
Of our midnight against the kitchen landscapes

Of childless times. Or did they exist at all?
Or do I? Or: do I dare not?
Your face floatfeeling in the lampbrown air
Wrenches free my distance
And I know now why
There is no land as
Nestled as light
In a reopened room.

A MOMENT

I need times like this to seed myself,
I need this: the coy wink of a season disjunct
When I can exchange my students for a rain morning
Or shut out a paper reading on a snow evening and
Crawl inward to the laboratory, the shelves, and nook
Of my fiber to contend without metaphor and manner
With life and death, to see that through one
That through the other I know. I love life and long
To live the quiet, the universal disseasonal,
The conceived seastruct of seconds. I cannot imagine
In autumn that leaves are dead: in all their color
They paint the day and harness the earth into centuries.

GHETTO MORNING

Day has stroked the window shade,
Seeping its touch along cracked veins
As if some finger had scraped away
Skinlike dark into this room shadowed
By you and me in a dead and juiceless color,
As a fruit before its fall. Under the wrinkled,
Wormlike shadows of the sheet our tired bodies
Jolt and grow unfamiliar

As if the cry of a bird with its head
Caught in thorns from a too fast
Flight was heard. But no tree drinks
Blood for you and me. It was only the street gleaners
In their garbage men attire mocking last night's napkin
With its lip transfiguration.

FIVE FINGERS

As if five fingers had been thrust before a flame,
As if from a hand stretching to some dark corner for a broom,
Evening descends in shades and shadows.
In light also to seem slow, naked, and undetected.

Evening descends
Evening descends
Moths sway into the naked gleams near potted plants and trees,
Our eyes squint with the change.
This is the illuminating hour,
When the clouds' edges remain jagged,
As if erased or smeared by nervous fingers,
When birds hang upsidedown in the air
With curled eyes and melted beaks,
When there seems to be no hour,
Only an inbetween
Knelling at our eyes,
And our ears stare out at the image of its song.
The centuries creep forward and backward
Like streets toward corners.

Evening descends
Evening descends
And we, with this evening's gong in our eyes,
Go past messiah hucksters
Who promise cheap cathedral jesuses and halfgods
To some indifferent synagogues
Where we must know the feeling of crumbling knees
Below stone statues
While in wait for the large bleeding streetcleaner
To make the sign of the cross in crimson colors.

SUMMER MOON

As we sat there with our backs against the moon,
Staring at the water lurking and sniffing
On the stone steps, our huge canvas
Was a breeze, water, and stone—congested
In our eyesight as the scent of sea.
For sound: the wind muffled
The water lapping at the soaked steps
Like the breath of an exhausted hound.
Our fingers caressed the wet animality
And coaxed it upon dry brick
Where it pouted in slow dissolution.

TIME AND PURPOSE

What can I remember
of the last book belonging to the
historysquatting pages
of this country when every day in the world
the earth is not evil, though there are
evil signals constructing a grammar of hate,
an identity that knows no freedom?
How can I say I apprehend
the pitch and stress and flow of duration?

Moments spacing imagination
create a concussion of images
that, like one's own baby's milky
breath, induces an incarnation
of time and sight, for beauty is
and does not be in death.

For man nor woman nor I
can still intentions to be,
for the purpose that is is
in all things eternally.
If I could love time,
fixing a death that was mine,
no man would see more in
his own hand pinching rhyme.
My eyes could find
as I touch the world in my mind.

I cannot but record the yesterwhen
we walked the door of her tiny heart
and slipped in the key of sighs
to bring her through to a start.
Tomorrow or the day after our fever must
match her intensity and be a heat of smiles,
for there is often much to pry us miles
apart.

AN AGING ALCOHOLIC

Divine order and human purpose,
   alcoholics aging,
    seeping warm, steal
    their way as a soaked helix
    of focused distraction
coiled around the human heart
into what we call the human soul.

Every office, institution a corporate entity:
a church, each higher purpose above
or below another purpose, each ideology
but a theology. Pick your ledge. Don't jump
off. Enjoy the height. Every height is but
    above or below another height.
Why am I wide awake at this hour
    of the morning night?
Persephone never cried over one thing
or another, but only over the loss
    of Earth
and the discovery of pomegranate seeds.
Inhumanity, when I think on it, drives
me mad, makes me sad, renders me
helpless, until I get it that every group
or individual is an Olympian of
    defeat
    deceit
    moral gain.

The sun does not fall right for me here. Exhume me
    here. Lift me up through
    those three heavy doors
    to your mouth.

A REQUEST FOR EXILE OR CHANCE

Fool me.
Lie to me.
Detain me here with a wistful unrealistic story
Over coffee or tea of oceans of forests cleansed
By waves of galloping winds, of a just world
That validates our tales and memories, of the disappearance
Of hunger, of where nature is kind and there is no need
Of heaven, nor mortal havens.

Our flaw is in seeking through the mass of contradictions
That every life creates for a single coherent myth, while
Ignoring my own insight is what I have just begged
You for. There would be no problem at all if among
Us our villages, towns, and cities did not harbor rooks
Where roost the imminent delusional, the imminent suicidal,
The imminent enraged conspiratorial, the imminent destroyer
                    Of lives.

How far are we good ones from being any different
With caved tunneling voices in our head? Are we
Different just because these bashedbrain conversations
Lead only to stillness and silence? Am I getting through
To you, America, or are you leading me astray?
Which of us is more isolated and shy? Which
Of us is the other's imminent paranoid? I do not
Foment wars abroad, nor deaths along the streets
And backroads of our wards and parishes. I cannot
Scratch a foraging finger across a globe and slip
An insouciant trigger fingernail hidden beneath
Any idle boulder or rock.

How unlike any individual is any nation? I feel guilt
For asking such questions in your head, for I need
To love my country even when it creates wrong
As well as right, whether it be precipitous or diffident,
In sickness and in health, for richer and for poorer,
Until death and resurrection depart, then reunite us.
We know from reliant books enough about royalty to know

That America, where man and woman, violent dreamers
That they are, believe themselves to be king and queen,
Though fortunate not to rely on dynastic rulers, nor on stoned,
Compliant, complicit, indifferent citizens who vote
Their hatreds. Have I buried prophecy here?
Lie to me.
Fool me.

AGING IN, AGING OUT

For a second there, I believed
You humorously meant birds.
But you meant, on non-analog leave,
Parachutists documenting the universe,
Strapped in a gravity belt and camera sill.
I was about to remind you birds
Have no apparent free will.
Then I got it, and chuckled.
Yes, I suspect many of us, born
A generation or so later, might be torn
Today between holograms and film.
The new technology in all of its tentacles
Invites us all to a pagination without fragrances.

More trees will live.
Each generation of young
Is at odds with an earlier one,
A sober ardor and ardent mind
Subtle in the blood. Unavoidable,
New unthinkable compulsions.
I am still seeking storytellers,
Their circles, their figures, their tones:
An emotional necessity awakened
By new needs.

Age always meets us halfway,
An excavation not of bones
Tearing through flesh an ancient sway
But of youthful galaxies of tombstones,
First and foremost, then of dust,
Copycat obituaries
Hardening as rust
At the predaceous day
Of the hour seeking stories.
Fragmentary, non-linear experiences
That the mind seeking traditions lies
About. Violence strives against this city's
Intrusive sincerity on arcade wings.
Barges still scale the river on commerce's belly.

OLD MANDEVILLE BY THE LAKE

Governed by rules brought into form,
Root, sprout, twig, trunk, branch, and limb,
Our planet once again is unstable.
In this century the jewels of its face
Acned by nationalist hates, its body
Cankered by the grace of the dates
Of years miscalculated by the greed
Of corpocratic oligarchs. From Form,
Form, perhaps even the universe in our
Chaotic hands is made unbalanced.
Around our wrists, sickened in the same
skin and uniform in the game, we wear
Bracelets and bands of tactics continuing
Tomorrow but never strategies toward glory
And equality.
           These are thoughts that juggle and tumble me
When I cannot figure out how to calculate
My own time and space in the world, nor
The awful significance of abandoned poor
Creatures among us. Where is the compass
To the new door opening above our heads
In the air to truer hearts to slip through?
Then again, escape is no solution;
The entire surface of the earth is a concentration
Camp unfixed by words, by words unpoemed.
All is incomplete. Language and the body politic
Do not connect in a city or church that pretend
To be neither a church nor a city.
           Born as children wanting to be different,
Some ignored the given and the placed. Now at even
An earlier age, newborns know the vagina as a bud
Toward bloom at the mere touch of intimacy. Each
Ejaculation a birth of galaxies. Which acts of ours
As a nation are worthy of treasury and blood?
           More an interior seeker than a wanderer outward,
Some of us cut away the fat in our arguments. Nonetheless,
Always puzzled, I confess I am, by people who renounce all
To gut-renovate a house or life to place their soul and will

On the altar, prayer rug, or dais of another: of a man or woman
Of the collar or cloth or high hat, of a section chief, dean or don.
How is it that most of us, each generation the last of a breed,
Come through anyway, as dreams are lost, never demanding
More? It must be that we age. Aging is not private, though,
Though an individual life can be: a slow gait of wrinkled skin,
Crinkled crow's-feet, the loss of hair, the proliferation of the chin.

ON BURIAL GROUND

I would not much like to leave this planet
Though this planet is leaving me. At seven
Through the brief slant of the upstairs blinds
The pines seem to be a gray piping against
Bright overcast sky where the faint flitting
Of a bird punctuates and creates the scene
With a golden thread in its beak. A life is forever.
Every word a trustworthy immigrant in exile,
Trustworthy in arms. Narrative is a bitch, as
Reason raids evolution designed with a wink
And wisdom of the intelligent gaze of the Sacred
And the Human on science and critical thought.
The truest teacher is here today and gone today.
Some of us mound a grave site for pets or cremate
Them, as if we were less important or not at all
Singular. On burial grounds where we are often
Born, even before Earth had a word for it, gravity
Was our first discovery as infants. The one gift
That makes of us a single hybrid presence. We fall
To earth, are tumbled to it when not burned under
Volcanic sludge or snow or at sea, or ash to ash
Sealed by love's remembrance in an urn.
It is how we get there through the secret heart of death
That is hard to swallow.

Flying blind in, through, and out of amplification vectors,
We have entered the girlization, the maidenization,
The parthenozation of our culture. It may turn out to be more
Salutary. No idea. Most men love things that break down: they
Can feel manly by repairing them. That's our PC generation.
The Mac generation, male or female, prefers to plug in and play:
No hassles where men and women are more drawn together,
Embraced by a techy heart. Take a long close look out there:
Men and women appear similar in cloth and laughter. We are not
Persuaded by the false fictions of tv and film drama. Dramedy
Is the new norm now, a new maiden voyage. Our physicists, guys
And gals, are all trying to be the new Columbus discovering
The outermost reaches of the galaxy. We are no doubt looking

At hubristic men and women looking for the Infinite and the Sacred,
Preferring to call It a secret, mysterious force field, and prefer not
To call it the Divine. Not that it matters. No matter how close they get,
There will always be something out there in the center of the dark,
Winking at us, waving us not closer in but farther out, and farther away,
Challenging us to come in.

AGON

> *A living thing seeks above all to discharge*
> *its strength——life itself is will to power*
> (Friedrich Nietzsche).

I

In a pick-up parked innocently vicious against the curb,
  Greatly out of sorts,
  A movie script shooting across a screen in his brain,
  Sanford's heterosexual, vengeful, macho, vigilant mestizo
    Citizen childlike stalks
    The gated air
    And street lamps
    Through his windshield.
The day hushed, backed into its darkening wardrobe.
  The eyes of day shut.
  The oncoming evening listened as it embraced
And snuggled within in wait for the night.
  The eyes of night refused to blink.

  George's jigaboo radar on annoyed alert
  For layabout outliers, owleyed,
Swiveled his neck left, right, and behind to scour
    Beyond.
Everyone this night will be pieces slipping like nails unrailed
  From the stigmata palms of angels.
Irritated, irritable, through the grove he hears hissing below ground of his
Voice and his wife's doubling back underfoot over stale ground and tales.
  They had fought and he hissyfitted away,
    Leaning into his anger and anguish, he
    Would be no sissy for no bleeding female,
      He swore, often as much.
From that evening on, his every evening unrequited would be premeditated.

II

A breeze as supplicant as Florida seedless satsumas palls the cobalt air.
  Trayvon flips his hood up.
  George scowls, then smirks, A hood in my hood in his hood.
O, Jack, what have they done to you?

A bloodstained Dallas echo whimpers
Back and forth across our map.
        In a nation whose members of Congress do not read its bills
They are content to lie about, whose ensorcelled citizens are eager to suck
The swords of lies down their gullible throats one gulp at a time,
                Dumbstruck awe arises from opinionated silence.
                This is a nation of deep-throated idiots.
                Shall I be vaguer so that you may understand?
Every one of us a continent unto ourselves has been stone nuts
Ever since our tonguetied bowels first grunted syllables
Of a falsehood about separate bodies and private minds.
Our lips, stammering and stuttering ever since have screamed
Unredemptive hatred across Africa, Europe, Asia, the Americas.
Tooth and talon, we have ripped to threads one another's flags,
Banners, and books; to dust each other's art and laws. Nothing
But a species alone, blind to the difference between seduction
And molestation, we choke off each breath of another.
Othering others, we other the selves of our lone humanity.
Trayvon and George are every continent, every language, every
                Burp, grunt, belch,
                Rape, and kiss.

Unleashed on highground on this Florida evening, up to his thighs in dark light,
Stroking his way home, Trayvon struts, bounds, and slips along past the lair
Of locked temples of joy toward his father's face. His pace unaware.
        I cannot be vaguer than this for you to understand.
                O, Jack, what have they done to you?
                O, Jack, don't you weep and moan.
                O, Malcolm, don't you weep and moan.
                O, Martin, don't you weep and moan.
                O, Bobby, don't you weep and moan.

George is surprised that Trayvon does not weave and bob.
                Nor does he slouch.
In a grim endurance of the moment, their worst natures
Will puff up and break forward through their breasts even
Before George steps manly onto the street. Their world
Is thinkable only by them. Neither is our victim or idol
To hold so dear to our breast. Each is but a nurtured target
                Of his own internal breeding
                And lack of evolutionary wisdom.

III
Trayvon
Loping across the highway, across the grass, tilts his head
Toward a shadow in its car as if staring to make sense of the face
Of a corpse in an open casket. Crazy crackers, lurking honkies,
Deceitful rednecks get you going and coming every time, he thought.
Trayvon
Perhaps had never heard of Mersault. There was no sun blinding
His way, no pistol in his fist. He had only open palms to ball
Into hammers or to curve into scythes. These two not yet boys
Into men, a veil twisted around their brain; sentinels invading
A self-imposed remorseless purdah of the spirit,
Inhabiting our stories without end, will not become leaders.
Each beside himself. Each without the courage to perceive
Consequences and to not condescend toward sacrifice:

> Each a reflection against a surface.
> Each a tangled thread swerving
> Through an entangled universe
> Hurled by dark matter, dark energy.
> Each lacking the fiercest compassion
> > To forgive the most unforgivable,
> > Their love of anger uncritical.

Their brutish cheeks smeared with the thinnest patina of belief.
A face against a table top, a piano top, a counter top, a bar top, a high hat
> A face against a pavement
Lap to lap, chest to chest, breast against breast, fists into chins,
> Pedophile against child
> Rapist against boy
> Palms to palms
> Fists gnarled by death, hijacked by a despotic brain
They but gravitate
Toward what tastes best to them: compulsive impatience and suffering.
> Dependent, co-arising,
> They do not exist because the world exists.
> Their world exists because they
> > *Intertwined are.*

Slipping into heat and madness, into the cummerbund of nastiness,
Easy Anger's twins, accusers in each other's face, stand their ground
Above a mournful heap of rotted black bodies now shrouded in suburban
Green where they rumble: one an instigator in his stance, an insinuator

Lurking behind his eyes. Another an instigator in his mere being; an
Insinuator with hesitant hands.

IV

G pulls his penis from his rectum and assassinates
                                The lad.
T slumps down between G's legs into his lap where he
                                Unarmed, undone, outgunned
                                Sighs into dying.
                                The night air
                        Sways   Swerves   Swoons
Gunpowder empires, for reasons that neither will understand,
Each might have judged the other and be judged by us as cavalierly
As the unconscious visitation of a bullet casing arcing in trifling
        Anger down toward the afternoon grass.
Crossing the memorial whirl and waves of infinite annoyance
                G will dance a two-step among his kind toward acquittal.
                T will brittle statuesque among our people toward innocence.
                                Yet
In our own anger and pain, in our own good health and joy,
                Sorrow, grief forever, and madness,
                                All
                                Of us
                                Each
Still may not understand that the tight corners we each occupy
                Are not as we are taught:
                                Separate,
                                Different,
                                Unique—
                                But instead:
                                Empty.

V

                Who owns the narrative
                To speak from a position of privilege?
Crossing as time and water cross dimensions
Calm and turbulent, we will never be sure
Of the answer, yet must ask:
                If they did not exist, what would we be doing?
                What would we be doing if they were not the case?

BUT NOT TO

Our cemeteries from Grand Isle to Natchitoches peered
Into the future from Land's End to World's End, shifted
Ground, and now beg for more graves to cement our losses.
Awe arises out of silence. When late August heat crosses
Over into early September, a loathsome, hideous swarm
Assaults my windshield bugged by accident by love.
                Well into September,
                Splat annoys my windows.
                Splatters, my grill.

      Can emotional intelligence be far behind?
What must it be like to a brain to be a brain? Is it the same
As to a muscle what it is like to be a muscle, or an eye to an eye?
                This is where the beauty lies,
                There in the middle, where
                                There are no predatory puzzles
                                To solve nor revisionist history to embrace

                                To disclose but not to reveal.
                                To suggest but not to explain.
                                To concede but not to discuss.

A PRAYER BOOK'S RESPONSE

To grasp the truth she needs to see her face
In the mirror above the sink on a hurrying train
As her shoulders jostle from wall to wall,
As she loses her step small steps by small steps
On the kiss slippery floor.

What is serious but nothing at all. It's all
A studious prerequisite to the next slipping
Away through the limen in the Veil,
As knowledge of the hymen disappears.
Only the body knows when, where, and how.
Relax and flow with the flow, we are taught.
Harmonious at the root, dissonant above ground,
Seizures abound in the brain.

How can we create a monastery or convent or ashram
Of the mind without stealing away from belief? Out there,
There in those places, there will always be others in the way.
We must learn to live on the edge between the ashram
And the non-ashram of our hearts. Volitional options
Do not exist. Our inner selves are but basement tenants
                    Or attic landlords.

She undoes the blue habit around her blonde hair, stuffs
It with her blue cassock and stockings and opaque
White blouse into a plastic bag to leave beneath her seat,
And dons a long sheer black evening dress and a sly red hat
That makes her bite her tongue and lip. He is waiting for her
At the end of the line, at everyone's last stop, with more
In his heart than the rings and flowers in his Ghanaian hands,
And a pearl necklace. His kisses will part her. Hers will root him.

Everything impermanent in our hands matters, is holy and sacred.

LIES INTRAVENOUS

Reading an oblique life of Freud, reaching for my coffee,
Looking up over the cup's rim, I spotted three of God's men.
One is in his collar and blue-gray cashmere sweater, long-sleeved;
Another, t-shirted and newly seated, fidgets with his papers of notes,
On this week's homily, no doubt; the third one, the more in our faces
Evangelical one, who roams about in soft, quiet polished brown shoes
From table to table through half the morning until someone's quiet,
Patient eyes suggest that he may plop his elegant ass right there
At heaven's gate.

At heaven's gate in earshot, soused with indifference and delusion,
he sermonizes all morning in his buttersoft hunter's drone, in his
Wildgame hat, his thin brown leather jacket, and postmodern spectacles
Resting on the bridge of his nose. His voice crosses each ridge of decorum
Toward the ceiling, high above the whistle and hiss of the Italian coffee
Machine. His once Catholic now Calvinist lips glisten with presumption.
I am not sure I like this preacher man. I spotted him once in the open air
At an outdoor blues concert and was glad he had not noticed me. Or had he?
Who was avoiding whom?

Who avoids whom? Avoiding no one, studying everyone, Freud
Was never underfoot as these men are, pretending to speak
For the downtrodden, the downdriven, the downcast who are forever
On their knees below all pulpits and niches. A couch is what they need,
An easy chair to lie back in to unwrap their mind of lies intravenous
                     There.

XI. THE BELUMMATI CANTATAS

ORPHEUS AT THE FRONT GATE

The one thing God cannot do, once
Taught the Rabbis, is create Himself.
Therein lies our panic, for we can, so
Instruct the Poets, create ourselves, also
Him. Therein rests our freedom.
As for me, I am only a stranger
With nomadic cognition and intuitions.
I am not a house clown for
A god, but am that rusty-dusty Black
Guy in the front yard, trying to kick
Open the gate leading out beyond
The plantation. But the slaves Black
And White even before they try to flee
Are already shriveling and withering
Into the dust, dirt, mud and muck,
Refusing to stand up and run with me.
                    I am
No Christmas tree ornament
In the window, no mezuzah
At the threshold, nor Easter
Egg hidden under a fence,
Nor a lamb or goat whose eyes bulge
In confusion before the mullah's blade.

I am the scramble for Africa backwards.
Clap!, went one hand once, perturbing
A battle aria among subatomic particles
Between matter and anti-matter at
The beginningless beginning, eons
Before the strewn of graveyards, where
At the center of billions of years later
Awareness and consciousness in intricate
Species evolved root and branch together,
Among trillions upon trillions of galaxies
Of worlds of universes, shaping cerebral
Weapons accommodating delusional
Thinking. All caused by the uncaused
Big Bang weird-wording the first unheard,

Unseen good news boom. So the scientists
Reveal to us. However, that's how gods
Create themselves: with helium and lithium,
Hydrogen and arguments, breath and answers,
Death and responses; with leaves, season-leaving,
Dying into color: a nested hierarchy of footprints
Approaching consciousness when awareness will
Possess indirect rule, finality, fun, and bugles will weep.

IN THIS YEAR

Note how tragedies vie for headlines daily,
Bullying one another to the edge of print,
Shoving each other over the edge of hoary
Memory. Old whores we are for mugging
One another's nerves with syringes
Of feckless news.

In years to come—I will not say centuries since
Stupid ideas are often displaced by more stupid
Beliefs time after time—we will remember in the
Days of Barack, Russian women are commanded
To wear only cotton underwear for fear of chafing
In anything else. In Turkey women are forbidden
To laugh in public lest they be deemed unchaste.
In America birth control is declared to be immoral
Because it aborts or second-guesses God's intention
For humanity. It is always about the vagina. In
Northern Nigeria men are enjoined to embrace their
Weapons and plow their women as their fields as,
So they say, Heaven commands.

Poverty, education, and war define our failures overall.
Nothing emanates outside of us on the planet without
Emerging first from inside. The planet first imagined
Is internally always us. Read the headlines:

*Man shot in head during traffic stop Monday; New
Orleans Police Department never publicly disclosed
Shooting.*

*Lower 9th Ward shooting has left 4-year-old blind, his
Brother with brain injury: grandfather says.*

*City of New Orleans gives homeless 72 hours to clear
Encampment under Lakeview overpasses.*

Black people in Ferguson are fighting for their freedom.

Britain, France, now Germany alongside, we may go
to war against ISIL—Saudi Arabia still won't commit.

Jordan, Syria, Lebanon don't want more Palestinians.

Byzantium king's tomb turning into Istanbul garbage dump.

Criminal acts by many from outside the state, Missouri
Governor deploys National Guard to Ferguson.

Ebola: A Humanitarian Crisis across West Africa.

Cable News Network tries to moderate a conversation about
the mental health of young men of color …. It didn't go well.

We turn away from headlines in grief or anger.
Don't we read?
Don't we want to read and feel?
Can we not see how
Events, incidents, and twists weaponize language
Entering the eyes and ears, sheering the hearts of
Ventriloquists sitting pretty on the laps of deadwood?

Selfful Robin Williams	a belt around his throat
Selfdied in the days	of Barack.
Brains like Robin's	will inhabit the future,
Until we learn	to harness the brain's
Battery to unignite	its endless misfiring
And the seashell	whispering hissing
In our ears	during　the night.

I pray that Heaven's and Hell's indifferent, disinterested
Love, though watchful and bemused as we trade barbs
And spill blood over banal heresies of our capricious
Imaginations for self-survival, will also pray.

In Ancient times long ago the involuntary observer on
My shoulder would have suggested that the dark we call
Night blocks the sun. It is not easy to know what disparages
The character of the day. In our lives lived in a pipe, tube,

Or tunnel, we are never angry for the reasons we imagine.
I hear the anger and the pain coiling up over the stories
Others and we tell. In this world, are we involved in a war
There, and here? What narratives are we missing?

It is very easy to despise humanity since there is no other
Sentient mammalian intellect to compare us to. We believe.

It's starting all over again. Perhaps we need do nothing.
Perhaps that is our missed purpose: that we need do
Nothing at all, ever, unto ages of ages.

It's starting all over again; in perpetual, not eternal, time:
Black and White perpetrators of our cities, towns,
And villages become younger and younger. Lacking
Humility and a Redeemer, we need do nothing as we do
Nothing at all.

I have passed through so many hallways, stopping in so
Many rooms, wondering, asking, What if we had done it
All differently? Would Sparta, Alexander, Caesar, Narmer,
Sundiata, Muhammad's Caliphs, Cingöz Khan, Osman,
Napoleon, Lenin, Atatürk, Bush, Putin, Erdoğan have molded
More creative orderless dominions?
Does destiny inhabit their names?

We are neither our minds nor our brains but something else
Hidden, sensed but unseen, felt but untouched, here but
Unexamined there. Our brilliance and our stupidity
Compete for our narratives.

At times I appear to lack footnotes on the tip of my tongue
Among borrowed Mayflower, Plymouth Rock scowls, grins
Or shrugs.

Actually, I spit them aside to feel free, to be free, distant,
And liberated. I will swallow stones four hundred twenty
Years old or more. Without the phenomenon of birds
Shaped by clouds intrigued by tales in children's books,
We would be joyless, foreboding creatures: weary stilts

In creaking clothing. Their mothers' wombs have prepared
Our youth to die. A democratic spring soon becomes
A fanatic zealot's winter. Only dreams restore dignity,
But evil also dreams,
As many are often
Reluctant to be seen,
As others live stream
Their own street attack
Over bling, a girl, or crack.

SKOPELOS

This is not a day for shaving.
Indifferent quilts of clouds
Graying purple, soused
By sheets of rain, mist, and fog,
Blow northward from breakwater
To breakwater the length of the island
Over wooded spines and hooded wings,
The forested knuckles of its hills
Hilling into mountains of pines and streams.

Tethered in the harbor under sweeping winds,
Sailboats, rocked, strain against the prevailing
Balance of the tides. Rolling waves of tomorrow
Or next week will surge forward, promising
Summer's sun, daylong cicadas, and sea doves.

I clutch my pillow to my slumbering dreams
Buried deep in a forgetful fit, scratching
At the surface of a mountain of mind, awakening
To the first day of an extended reaction vacation
Promising lamb baked in plums and the gleam
In a glass of throat-soothing tsipouro or gin.
Neither day nor night will vacate
Or abandon songs. The poems of birds
And flowers merit the Aegean's
Morning and evening twilight.

Greece is a country of island nations,
Each nation an island or inland country
Unto itself beckoning me to come back
Once again as a visitor strolling into
The future, and to stay forever.

ALONISSOS

At Steni Vala where monk seals once swam
Unmolested for centuries, I wonder how
The world, blinkered surely, will respond
Today from its knife edge to learn had Adam
Of our myths only questioned in the very
Moment of the naming what kind of world
We would be. Even though perhaps still
In bits and pieces, if he had only perceived
The uncreated brain would create a mind
Seeking unceasing to recreate emblematic you,
Instantaneous me: perpetual Self's selves,
Mind after mind, after mind. Mind-self after
Mind-self; god after god, after god, after
Adopted god? To preserve and sustain
The god of survival. Adam Mankind lost us
All reproduction rights in a fierce forest mist.

Form without detail. Form as itself. Form as self.
Conscious form without tail. Self-conscious tales
Of what is not. Do I have the courage for ridicule,
For disdain? And what of Hellas and Asia Minor,
Where the grace of the embrace of tectonic plates
Over and under one another left at the center
Of Earth space for further stone carnality and
Untold springs to seep upward into new seas
And oceans without the aid of wet nurses or men?
Emptying upward is at the center of origin.

Of Alonissos, where African and Asian homeopathy
Offer up healing once again, rising awakened from
Forgetful memories, where boat captains' and harbor
Agents' wives cull old stories, are they lying to me here
In the square above calm over hills sloping toward forests
                    Or am I
                    Lying when I see
That imperialist mosquito there, lighting from somewhere
Off on a listless breeze through my villa window, fidgeting now
On the tip of my fingernail typing across the keyboard,

Riveted there riveting me, gazing left and right at letters
Crawling across my screen's bright light? What of it?
What has this sudden overbearing girlish insect on the roam
To do here with my sense of self? There are promising
Implications on the other side. Why do such notions come
To us? I do not live within knowledge of the precise,
Measured perturbation of our universe. It is but four billion
Years older than when our own old Earth banged about into
Existence. We live nowhere near the center of our universe
That may be but a mere outpost among trillions of universes
Out there beyond here. What do we know of there and here?
I know we need to uncover what is unknown. The worst
Of us spare lives. The best save them. I must not smash
This mosquito, but shoo it off as it transfixes me at bay,

>If I am fast enough either way.
>Yet I know what I do perceive
>I become.
>So come.

SKYROS

Skyros reflects human desire for insular isolation. Islands also
Are sentient. Whatever vain and violent happens, we call
History and history entering time unfolding always surprises.
I daily sit at the linenwrinkled shore of the fabricating bluegreen
Aegean silk shining out toward the purple horizon over
Sun mingled waves between earthquake mangled mountainsides.

The sense of wonder alone
Whether this *that* or that *this*,
Exists, is worth the cost
Of not knowing.

> Islands at ease encourage
> Fear of becoming
> Someone's biography
> Other than one's own.
> How must we stop
> The process of being
> Understood by misapprehension?
> We must choose the process of being
> Over an aloof fear merely to be.
> These were conversations I once had become
> Too impatient to make.

Nations are like that, too, never ceasing some process
Of matter and energy, space and time, mind and brain;
Of the sly, smug death of billions by billions over endless,
Uncountable eons. We are like that: we kill or murder
The self by slaughtering our own kind and one another.
We are a species ever at, in, and with each other as Source.
As each is one's own autobiographer, so are we every persons'
Mirror biographer. Disbelief is irrelevant.

Like islands, we occupy the maps, even as we flow,
Float, bump into one another, sometimes before handshakes.

JUST BELOW THE SKULL

We do not value reliability the way we used to.
Perhaps we try too hard to read, power-reading books,
Newspapers, and magazines throughout the day or
Evening for fear of missing out on planetary news.
We should go cold turkey on all periodicals altogether.
But can we, in fear of missing out? The more we read
Or watch or listen, the more ambiguity and frustration
Grow. What is out there can't be absorbed fully. Going
Cold on all news, internet aggregations, and blogs,
We can use the extra time during what is left of one's life
To live without beliefs and guesses to read
With greater certainly and easier care
Evolving texts of literature and science.

Imagine the gain in admitting that we haven't a clue
About what is going on anywhere, about much
Of anything, especially in politics and spiritual
Piety crossing the faces of those who disagree
With us whom we disappoint. Should we make
An exception of the slippery slopes of the arts
And sciences? Dare we even try? Every other
Month or so, to get our lives back,
        We can remain in the here now and then. Or read
        Only foreign books with a dictionary straight
        Through. What was it? Cable TV or the smartphone
        That led us to this point? I think the culprit was
        The buzz and tingle of electronic bloodletting
        And irony of ironies we moved even closer
To periodicals, especially since we could read them
As hardcopies, read them digitally, and even print
Out and save articles from them saved on a laptop.
I bookmark everything, save everything in e-folders,
Save everything in desktop folders, occasionally
Copying and pasting to a Passport
        Or Time Machine for Mac, and also to an external
        Hard drive. I bet I even have duplicates or triplicates
        Of stuff I forgot I had "saved." Saved! Ha! Cyberspace
        Is not reliable yet. It can all go Poof! A Cyberpoof

Is now a natural disaster, like Federal floods
Or hurricanes, or earthquakes, or mudslides.
The 'Net has imprisoned us. Driven hard into Cyberspace
Is no good for caged-up words. Driving words into cages
And boxes turns them into witnesses and suspects shackled
In an encased interrogation room. Cast out external drives. Let
Space in. Only Space. Tear down walls!

Unconvinced, yes, I throw away nothing. I trust Future
Archeaocyberchologists. Our choices forced upon us,
Nativism or indifference, have been cemented into
The walls of caves for what will seem like an eternity.
But I have confidence in us all. Once searching one's
Genealogy across thousands of years through DNA
Testing becomes inexpensive, more and more
Of us will discover longdead unknown blood
Cousins across a few ethnicities, tribes,
And civilizations. Africans, Europeans, and Asians
Have been boiling sperm and ovaries in a cauldron
Of genes in an enormous broth over uncountable
Millennia, mostly through love, lust, rape, and pillage.

A larcenous nomadic Ape just below our skull,
Tethered there, masturbates still, out of range,
Against human memory.
Soon members of the military will be panel controllers:
Air Traffic, Ground Traffic, Ocean & Sea Traffic. PTSD
Will develop from staring bleary-eyed at the screen as one
Pushes buttons and toggles over cities to destroy thousands

At a distance as if they were just around the corner.

WHERE OUR LAIR LIES

I suggested we stand outside
In the warmth of the sun just
Beyond the entrance, since we
Were leaving the hospital anyway,
Returning every second and fourth
Saturday of each month, to pore over
Sacred Aramaic and Syriac texts on
Unconditional sacred love with twenty
Or more others like ourselves, seeking.
       His inner ambiguous child always
       Shone through womanish eyes
       Beaming from his fetching male
       Smirk: his cultivated satyr's beard,
       Ragged eyebrows, and left ear,
       Pierced through by dangling gold
       Rings, like an extra smile or wink,
       Just in case one looked away.
Nodding toward the wing where our lair
Lies, Why do you believe I'll never be
Convinced, I ask Juice, by what we are studying
Here in our group? Sometimes he wants to be
Called Juice. Ace other times. At times, Deuce.
There is also Jules underneath.
       With so many mortal earthquakes
       Around the globe, it seems frivolous
       To be having this conversation. British,
       Russian tensions boil over again. Hungarian
       Fascists attack gay activists. the Taliban
       Reëmerge. Israel's forever accused of
       Erasing memories in Palestine. Jordanians
       Divide over the West Bank, yet war's
       Undeclared with ISIL. Black coaches seem
       To be far too fewer than white ones in
       South Africa. Besides, Tuesday will soon be
       Fat. So who's got time in New Orleans
       To swallow life's poisons? We just moaned,
       In fact, and mourned
The passing of Big Chief Bo Dollis.

Coming to town for JazzFest is Lenny
Kravitz. Never leaving town, thankfully,
Are Dr. John, Deacon John, Trombone
Shorty, and the graveled voice's
Ivory smile of Satchmo's spirit being.
       We intend to take off for Greece in a year.
       My wife suggests to bail. I would say to sail,
       To light flightful like Ikaros along the West
       And East coasts of the Aegean. But I still hold
       On to this moment with Juice in the warm sun
       At the entrance, or exit, if you will, of the hospital
       About Being and being convinced or not. Gratefully,
       The day was not hot and I was in no mood to go back
            In for
          A coffee and chat.
          This chat had to be
             Without.

IN AN AGE OF PLASTIC

> As disobedient as unnativist plastic is, so is
> Indigenous oil, swirling by force from its
> Natural layer through cold, dollar driven pipes
> Across desert and green, below clear waters,
> Veining and fracking Earth's womb from
> Canada to the Gulf.

Toxic British Petroleum Oil pees, spits,
And spills into our Louisiana dreams still,
Soaking through the gills, feathers, and wings
Of river life, lake life, and all wildlife that lights
Now upon quick silt and custardthick black water.

> The British chew grit and may never
> Decamp. Why would a judge, an Obama
> Nominee, a wisdom descendant of Solomon,
> Have dismissed the people's lawsuit against
> These pikers? Though Big Dirty Oil has admitted
> Fault, not even the pillars of science, the judge
> Ruled, in a state whose schools don't believe
> In science, can tell us who caused erosion
> Of our wetlands. Yet America has choked off
> The lifecycle of millions of Monarch butterflies,
> Their milkweed homes, food source, and nursery
> > Awashed in herbicides.

Artificial Intelligence today degrades and annoys
Users. Complex systems fused as smartphones
Churn up annoying bugs. We are very far from
Creating self-directed machines as smart as us.
Imagine complex algorithms that cause unstable
Stock markets. Imagine replicating

> > Circuits out of whack in our car's system
> > That cause accidents. Imagine unimagined
> > Estrogens and entheogens in our food chain.

Ours is the Age of Plastics. The age of digital
Provocateurs whose weaponized finger bears
Down on an unreliable keyboard interfacing
Irresponsible drone controls over our city parks
And college campuses. We have become a people
For whom Truth is never promising. So how can

We ever be convinced of anything? A part of our lab
Research is to de-weaponize the egg sacs of pesky,
Virus-bearing female mosquitoes. We will strive at it,
As once did Leander Perez of Plaquemines Parish, who
Bribed white male gynecologists to sterilize Black women,
To drive down Louisiana crime rates, he snapped.

HISTORY AT AN ANGLE

There is not enough tragedy and oppression
In America for Americans to discover a love
Of endless poems. Songs and movies replace
A need for succinct vision, voice, and feeling.
Songs reveal losers; movies, winners and deadbeats.
      We capture heroes in film, the universal
      Language against threats. Ourselves
      In photos, the universal language against
      Harm, we frame family and friends. From
      Art we learn to smile, laugh, think, and cry.
      Redemption slams into our lungs when we
      Realize the imminent end to innocence,
      Winded, struggling to catch our spirit's
      Breath in the midnight air above our gaze.
          Where are our twins,
             Marooned by households of
Predators and perpetrators; warriors,
Heroes; mothers and heroines; fathers,
Providers? There never was a chance
We would not have been dying forever.
As I am guessing, all is very much over,
Nonnegotiable, and unsalvageable for us.

It was a mistake to think that time, as well
As space, was a friend, even of itself.
All conditions and inhabitants of cycles
Move on as transformations meeting challenges.
Otherwise, how could we ever angle history
Looking forward?

CLEVER, CLOTHED

Waking from an unneeded nap, a talk show
On the radio drifting in from a distant room
About another new novelist's much touted book,

One has to have a new idle mind to love time
To imagine unmet needs of life without rhyme
To notice the swift shadow of wings fluttering

Across the trunks and limbs of tall pines of an
Eagle gliding on the currents of wind to its rook.
A recent find in the badlands of Eastern Ethiopia,

A jawbone in the Afar savannah of the East African
Rift Valley, clocks a *Homo* fossil kinship in at about
2.8 million years ago; most likely about the time

Adam and Chava became self-conscious and clever
Enough as Mankind and Life to don fig and sweet
Gum leaves, at the sudden startling mercy of mismatched
Weather.

I am speechless today. Time may give me words.
What do we accomplish on a planet where
Appeasement has led us to genocides, holocausts,
Wars, slavery, and, finally, death? What startling truths
Might we discover about our American lives if we only
Dwell on our loincloths of leaves?

The present is always future.

THE NAMED

At this unbound sheet of paper
This Turing Machine we now
Call a computer, a laptop, a smartphone,
I remember friends:
                    I think their names,
                    Intone them in my mind,
Rather than draw the attention to myself of unbelievers
Surrounding me by pronouncing their names too loud.
                    They must not be cursed.
Often laughed at, ridiculed, made fun of when
                    We were young, by one another,
                    Calling each other out of our name.
Fruittrapp! Whirliss! Orphlee! LilBro!
So I wish Katz's corner bar across Baron's Corner grocery
The sky's Peace upon them.
                    Grandfathers taught
That Peace is always at the feet of our mothers
                    Who taught and punished us.
I always insert the Blessing of Peace always when
I very infrequently evoke their names. My name must not be
Invoked overmuch, the American in me has realized,
Lest it become stale in the mouths of believers and in
The ears of unbelievers.

Fruittrapp, Wallace, Whirliss, Orphlee, TiBro, Elmo,
Roy, Lawrence, Gerald, Orland, Elmo, Clarence, Bobby,
Donald, Claude, Otis, Mark, Samuel, John, Don.

                    American Prophets are not automatons.
Their intoned words gifted directly
Are too holy and sacred to be repeated robotically
As if we are caught in the center of some autistic trance,
                    Bobbing up and down
Over Holy Ground; or falling into trance in windowless lodges.
More like Sangha Buddhists; or like Anatolian Sketes,
We are
                    Locked in and out of inward prayer.
                    All of that will really belong to us again some day.
                    Their Spirit, our Spirit, has deemed it so.

THE SYSTEM

Haman Reincarnate has become our new President.
We need more than ever before more brave, fascinating
Cohorts, those with a holistic perspective and an ethical
Mind, a sustainable consciousness as the sciences
Of consciousness suggest. Such minds are mostly excluded
From American politics and government. Nor are they very
Popular in the rest of the world's governments, either.
Especially not in free cultures.
Indeed, culture is stronger than the Holy Word.
Only the Lodge of the Four Sabbaths will transform
A wrongful world of a dying planet.
Whom might we elect as leaders who will untether
The evolution of our societies, managed altogether now
By shadow states, who finance elections as power struggles?
There is global collusion among the world's 1%:
The ultra-statists, who are essentially stateless,
Who control the financial markets, and thus governments,
Through the buying and selling of companies, insurance,
And distant silver-spoon estates.
Local politics are a supported circus.
The managed media keep us focused
On the surface.
We may as well enjoy the game, but shouldn't get
Too attached to the results of insults.
Dialogue is possible only when those
In power nowadays lust after it.
Perhaps my life is only in the bend of its evening.
We have no way of knowing. Let us caress all curves!
I see this increasingly and selfishly as no longer my
Problem, however.
Neither in the sense that I don't spend so much time on my digital
Devices, nor that I'm at the tail end of my life. I see the human race
Continuing on its merry way along the edge of the abyss with the usual
Alacrity and abandon. Better to die in a car while on the phone than on
The streets with a gun pressed, smirking, between our eyes. Not
Much better, but a little so, because we are not then left to another's
Devices.
My neighbor dislikes Jews less than he dislikes other groups.

Would you call him an anti-Semite? Can an anti-Semite still be
Someone who dislikes Jews just a little bit? I suspect most
Russians dislike Jews, especially those like Putin who have
Rediscovered the Orthodox faith of their ancestors. Just as
There is a prayer among Orthodox Jews thanking God
For creating them men as Jews and not women, there is a
Passage in several Orthodox Christian liturgies about the Jews
As betrayers of Christ that also beseech Christ to protect
The nation's leaders and military
"Against all enemies."
What is it that's eating away at me?

I have listened in on several congregations of several faiths
Over the years of my life to know that they all make me very
Uncomfortable. Sometimes I imagine that my paternal
Grandmother is still whispering in my inner ear
Against the woman from whose womb I slipped.

    The system as
Corruption—corrupts, as a German Socialist professor teaching Bertolt
Brecht and Friedrich Schiller told me once, in my formative years.
Ben Carson doesn't seem to understand that Saul Alinsky was not
      Quoting Lucifer
But was instead quoting himself on the Lucifer factor in government,
Which he insisted needed to be fought from outside the system. For
What it's worth, Hillary Rodham felt and feels that it must be crushed
By working against it within the system. Alinsky knew that corruption
Corrupts; so he stood outside of it to crush it. The rest is still history
In the making. Haman and Clinton are in the system our brains embrace.

AN ALGORITHM'S POEM

Life like prayer eats at the human heart.
          Who says that?
          Did I or did I steal it from some place?
          These days I forget the names of plants.
Ligustrum. Acacia. October Daisy. Hydrangea.
          Hydrangea reminds me
Of my favorite cookie of my childhood: Hydrox.
          Better than oversweet Oreos, anytime.
Apart from the sail-swept sky toward the horizon out,
          I spy the curvature of doubt, soul, and self.
As a child in short pants, I believed only whites were
Catholic or Jewish. I felt invocations won't ever work for me.

Katrina God Damn! I miss those flambeaux lights that once
          Surrounded me in my youth and young manhood.
          Sweating during Carnival chilled winter evenings,
I have come to earth shorn of belief's discipline; one small
Hand clutching the other one, so they tell me, the right the left.
How many algorithm poems do I have in me? You heard
From my daughter I have some poems but we see nothing,
          You chortle.

Let me remind you: It is in a restful afterlife and peaceful
Territory beforehand that they slaughter one another just
Because they have different beliefs of what happiness
Will be like when they die. They maim and flail, ever so
Slow at it, in order to die off others quickly and first.

Truth be told: Nothing will ever change until women lead,
An electric socket in one breast, a bee's sting swollen on
The other, Natural Selection and genetic mutation's final
                    Makeover
                    Takeover.
Already some fathers, escaping through disconsolate clouds
And venerable sunlight, prefer to forget the past they abandoned.

I have privately believed there should be no separation between
Text and History, and believed that History is what re-emerges

Throughout time, Time Past and Time Present.
       I hear you often wonder why so many waste time
       In endless moments with useless shticks. I know why:
       So that the weird and wonderful won't become routine,
       And won't come so
Fast that they overwhelm us. We already
Unconsciously know that, of course, but most of us
       Rattled by others who distract us never turn away
       Toward and into our own consciousness to know
       What was or is truer. Here's another one: What makes
       These idiot politicians of ours—including store, bar,
Hotel managers, and religious nutters—think that a person who
Was successfully transitioned physically will be recognized as
What they no longer once were? It's as if they believe that
A transgendered person and a transvestite are the same.
Such inane fear and loose screwyness beget fulsome hatred's
                Repression.

TIDES OF MIND

Every day I dig I am alive.
       The roots of oppression
       To the spade and shovel
       Will give way.
The misfortunate of the world
       Believe every man coerces
       His inferiors and bends his
       Knee to his superiors.
It will always be so: the same
       Bowl of ice cream
       The same pie crust
       The same stale coffee
       And pale tea.
The young will even the score
With guns against their own,
For they hate themselves
For being hated in perpetuity.
I speak of the misfortunate ones,
Not those born to privilege unearned.
The debauched, dissipated illiterate
Cower no longer, rising up to murder
The daughters and sons of blind
       Witless good behavior.
Every day I dig I live,
Scraping aside
       On unprepared ground
       The excrement
       The defilements
       Of the walking incontinent.
Perhaps we inhabit the wrong world, not
The world of threads of high energies, of
       Twists, turns, and accidents
       Looped around strings of forces
       We cannot see twenty-seven
          Pilgrimage
       Dimensions out, constant
       By gravity, over prickly, smooth
       Warps and ripples, forces of tiny

Distances: a physics with unseen
Reason.
Great conflicts of history will rise,
As preludes to whose conquests of which
Cities? Where will the next New Worlds
Surprise?
Every day I dig I am alive, I live.

BRIEFLY HARBORED

On a Sunday afternoon
not quite the end of time

the air probed by indecision
hesitated in architectural briefness.

Spiritsharp, I viscerafused felt
a wave of ambivalence crest

astronomical through the pores
of this loneonce moment, then float

up and away as a test at capturing
the single second that humanizes

tourist shops of airports squatting
countrycornered against city currents

at the edge of dimensions
circling out from eye to ear:

as if time itself could beast the day
into birth

as if lands and machines could ripple and whinny
to life.

I have entered the unspoken exchange of cities
and slouched among the runic chairs of waiting gates.

The planes, iconic beyond window panes,
crouch passive among the hands

of the ground crew refueling with an interior tuning
to the hourly litany. I thought the beasts watchful,

human, capable of embracing minds and bodies across
the mileful skies. I knew that this was all

my imagination but that without it
all things still would come alive.

THE ANCIENTS

So much of life,
            More than we know,
                        Tethered,
Is the creation and work
Of the sublime, pummeled
Often by unrepentant clichés;
Of descending muses soothing
Our brain, nerves, and heart
In alto, tenor, and bass voices.
            The Ancients
Of Africa, Europe, Asia Minor,
            Occasional losses,
Though, would not have believed
                        In many
                        Gods
            For no reason at all.

Those ephemeral unseen vibrato
            Mouths of myths,
            Without motive,
Subliminal all the days of our lives,
                        There,
Right where we need them most
When even if we do not know it, are
                        Destined
To lead, guide, and caution us
                        Against
                        Or with
Our slumbering or awakened will.

Notice the catch we pivot and net
Or the prey we scout and trap
            In a blind stare.

The Ancients will.
We are what they and we ensnare.

The mountains we trek. The skies we
Soar. The museums we visit. The cafes
And pubs we savor for hours on end,
If not days. The books we discarded or read
          And retrieved from the trash bin.
          The books we forgot we had.
          The films we forget we ever saw.
The moments a thing got stuck in our craw.
          The voyages we imagine
          Or have taken before
          After retirement
                    Or dying.

          Tethered.

          Remember.
On towers, steeples, minarets, roofs
A god, an angel, a bodhi will.
          Real or imagined,
Ancients dwell within us still,
However not-knowing we may be.

THE SPONTANEOUS DJEMBE AT JAZZFEST

Sometimes I believe New Orleans is the last station
Stop before Nirvana, once JazzFest erupts and quakes
In miscegenated rhythms carnal, mystical, compassionate,
Forgiving the very unforgivable where music exists
Between the notes and in poetry between the words:
Each syllable liquid, fluid, and unleveed, a deep well
Of meditations yet undreamed; dreamed, yet unspoken.
Cadences yet unheard, yet sensed by the subtle body
                    Immortal
                 Where time does not exist.

I have never anywhere before JazzFest relished so many
Black, Brown, Red, Beige, White youthful, adultful bodies
Trembling to the djembe under Black palms, as if each one,
Abandoned, volunteers to the moment serving at her own last
Rites of passage, where colors of the body's largest organ have
            Escaped at last to freedom's will and song
                 In the female dancing.

THE SECOND LAW OF THERMODYNAMICS

Violence contains order, even as it visits disorderly.
At times, language never seems to rescue us.
   I don't know if I would have made
   A good, or even decent, chemist.
As a child I soon lost interest in the chemistry
Set I had, where our front porch was my lab, my lab
   Stool the stoop of steps toward the front
   Gate. Not knowing nor understanding what
I sensed I should already know or understand at ten,
   I simply gave up before scarring myself,
   Or the painted wood of a splintering gray porch.

   I know we live in an ambiguous world.
   I have known condescending decent people
   Who remind me so: the principal of a school
   That never would have admitted us yet,
Who mistrusted Martin Luther King. She ruled
Him a Manchurian Candidate because of his slanted
Almond-shaped eyes pressed between a thick forehead
   Deep above a balcony of cheeks: A Chinese
   Mole or quisling, she guessed. When I visited
Back home three years later, from Tunisia and then Paris,
I found in her a staunch, admiring believer in King, and a
Supporter of school desegregation, already ten years under way.
   Citizen Council Spies, releasing fear, can evolve, I suppose.
   Or when statues speak.

Very much later, an older student of mine shared with me she,
Her husband, and neighbors, because of unrelenting New
   Orleans street crime wanted to
   But would never
   Vote for David Duke
   To become Governor
   For the fact that he
   Hated
   The Jew.
Was it her vote or mine that saved Louisiana that time?
   A silent looking on of peoples' twisted fears,

I said nothing,
Except, "Yes, I see what you mean," when she asked,
"Do you
See?" I had neither the heart nor the patience
To let her know had Duke loved Black People
More and hated only Jews, still—still I would
Never vote for him. One day I may tell her so.
The school principal died long ago.

At every intermission the American Culture evolves at warp
Speed. My generation of acquaintances and friends now occupy
A cautious questioning territory of deliquescent perennial leftovers:
A tendency of remission as they hide from old age in plain sight.

A new Ottomanmania lurks Asia Minor, still seeking at a gallop
A Turkic Monolithic Identity, suppressing difference; its thundering
Hooves stomping into the dust the throbbing, breathless eternal
Heart of Anatolia. Turkey's interloper's lathered heart never seems
To recognize its friends and allies: Back and forth it embraces Syria,
Then Saudi Arabia, then Iraq, and yet again Iran. In Iraq it slaughters Kurds
And leaves alone ISIL. In Syria it slaughters ISIL and rides over Kurds.
The enemy of my enemy is my enemy,
Nationalistic religious Turks imply.
The White House, confused as England and France of the past,
Bows to a Nationalistic Neo-Ottomanmania. "Surely this will come
To no good," David insists. "Why would they open up a two-front
War, let alone support it, when, as you have implied to me, for them
The enemy of my enemy could at least be my temporary friend?"

I recall a conversation at Jamila's
Over Köfte, Merguez, and Couscous, shortly
After returning from Turkey in 2007, with
An American widow whose husband, a Kurdish Iraqi Jew,
Had died some time ago. She did not understand what all
The fuss was about with Palestinians since life and history are
Indifferent to nations: states invade states: that is what they do: people
Are disbursed or sent on long marches Southward. "So they need to get
Over it! Move on! We all need to get over it!" her pale skin grimaced.
"We need to move on. Or we have no core.
"It happens to us all, century after century."

I had never thought of *it* that way before and sensed there is some
>> Comfort in realizing Life
>> Is cyclical, not linear.
> Leo later at our favorite coffeehouse countered the widow's lack
Of wisdom: "Anatolia as before!" he punned. "It is still more than ever
Our duty to avoid repeating the worse things we have done to one another:
Genocide, wife beating, slavery, rape, over and over again. That is something
>> In
>> Our power."
I believed then and now
>> We sons need daughters, our
>> Emanating manifestations, as
>> We each unwind from the spool of history.

SIX LINES ON TRUTH

The City can do no more,
And if it can do other,
It can unfold butterfly or flag,
Or coil in, pyramiding:
Exclusion, dismissal, evasion, void.
In a walk's distance there is death.

Or
The truth stands by itself.

XII. UNBIDDEN I TURN

FISHERMAN WITH NO HANDS

Puffs of clouds sulked into form
As feathers of a wing seamed by bones
Into the body of a bird
As if to pull the world into the sun and sea.
     The wind moaned and ripened,
     Husking from an animal's throat,
     Loping barebone across pebbles
     In a slow gathering of riot
     Into the thoughts of a fisherman with no hands:
     With eyes of a fish chasing through lost sight out of water,
     His thoughts nudged in grains of sand for lack of hands.
     Wind came like dry rain,
     Sogging his oldman body;
     Water came in wind upon the sand,
     Shriveling away from images made by others' hands.
     Waves turned under and were lost
     As sounds of fishermen's hooks grappling upon sea rocks
     Until midget waves as if great limbs
     Scampered to the toes of his bare feet.
His breathing was flesh,
Behind some strange rib
In a sense of body,
Feeling the thought, the presence,
And taking it.

     It rains and solemnity flows from the eye
     In effort to stretch, scatter, and strain
     Through a world of days in sun
     And nights in stars whose breath is silence,
     Light, and rain. Pour, rain, pour
     With your own sound, make
     His mind wonder what it is
     To be a drop of rain quenching
     The world upsidedown along twigs, conjuring
     The chill of damp sap in the skinspringy grass
     Until the sun recognizes the ends of trees,
     The gray, bare bark of woods, the wet of leaves
     In the soundless dip of brass. Pour, rain,

Wear away roofs in tin time,
Stutterstep across any toil, dance
And smooth the dents of soil
Before flowing to gutters. Rinse the eye,
Stone to stone, reminding earth
Once cause was meaning:
While rain is puddles and sea.

Somewhere off thunder bellowed
As quiet lightning blinked
And opened and closed the clouds.
Water tingling between toes
Caught the moment of fishermen's twine
Cutting foamy white palms descending
To the pews of paws and knuckled rocks.
The cuffs of his sleeves hung unbuttoned,
The wind bruised the sewn skin.
What deciphers
The alienation of a leaf or
The beginning of a star?
But let me speak to it.
To something whose delicacy
Is death in a wrinkled hand,
A bird dying in an old man's palm,
Or nestled against a woman's breast,
And then I will know it is time to draw
Away from the land,
Clenching a fist,
Hammering the air once, twice.
I will know it is time
To let men in ships go starward
From Earth
While I on Earth pester my own old, present time
To help me bring up the back in thought,
While under a bridge a frog
In search of earth and water
Squats his lumpy body in a grassy gutter
Squashes the roots beneath the rising puddle.
Some lakes quench their beginning from rain.
Others murmur up from soil.

Either can make a man or woman
No matter their thirst or worth.
Every man has been wet with time. But rendered wet once,
One can hardly say it has never stormed
Or that he has never been soaked
Alone
During
An ending chime,
A ship's clanging bell,
Evenings
Descending
Anyway.

THE EYES OF I AM

Who is to blame that we lit by indifference show little
        Interest to those around us?
They also are muqaddas, kadosh: holy, different, separate,
        Unique. What explains our shunning

Off? No life ever matters until the whole nation
        Recuperates dignity in the margins.

Where might we look for light?
        Certainly not among frumpy
Frostbitten speeches, nor among
        Meddling quarrels with the self.

Beyond designated space and roles
        Assigned, something new comes,
Creating us creating it. Something
        Inside us has shifted agitations,

Enticements, frequencies, and vibrations.
        We are already the best we can
Be. Believing we can amount to better
        Betrays the faithful self always there.

We are in a time of great change
        And possible transformation.
Why come down on the side
        Of the darkest of probabilities?

If I enter an unlit room to look through
        The window from a middle distance, will
I see in my past everyone who stands
        Or sits here before me now? If I move up

Closer, will I see more, seeing there more
        Clearly? What do Americans' eyes tell Americans'
Brains? Others to the contrary, I, rootless, am
        Comfortable being uncomfortable in the midst.

What we leave behind is not our worry, neither
        The space nor the time nor the flaws nor the problems.
As we leave the planet, we neither need to forgive
        Nor accuse. Strange that such sheer freedom comes

Only at the end. What's even stranger is that I don't
        Know what I am talking about. I guess talking will
Also be unnecessary during our conscious or our
        Unconscious-conscious ending. I must confess I do

        Not understand the dictator's heart. Why
Did Stalin purge, vanquish—and then put down—
        Trotsky, Kamenev, and Bukharin? Why were
They enemies of ideas to him? Despots murder loyalty

        To an idea itself as an enemy of the people, the state,
The leader's person itself. I am Hitler, Golda Meir, Stalin, Svetlana,
        Trotsky, Mao, Khomeini, Cengöz Khan, and every
Enslaved Middle Passage captive and slaver and enslaved.

        I Agonistes must proceed, preceding.

        By acceptance of self, of love of self—forgive
Ourselves of the personal, recalled memories needing forgiveness.
        Kiss the need with fearful lips to forgive others. When called
Upon, devour the need to guide others toward forgiving themselves for being

        Victim and victimizer, predator and prey. The truer
Act of forgiveness is to forgive the truly unforgivable. Predator,
        Forgive your Interior Predator. Prey, forgive your
Interior Prey. The truest act of forgiving is self-forgiveness. Orbiting

        One another, channeling Agonistes at the Gates
Of Headstones, I and you, we and us, no longer matter and need not
        Reestablish traditional values endlessly.
        Embrace reverse-projecting. Oh, my eyes,
Is the left hand closer to the heart? I am. You Are. You are I Am.

        Before me, you were. Before you were, I am.
        Neither with withering disdain, nor moral dithering,

I no longer matter.

I no longer matter.

>Devastation felt by moral-ordered human beings
>Will not overcome an autocratic automaton, a robot
>>Not given to
>>Auto-annihilation.

BEING AND MEANING

Here we *are*.
What does it
Mean *to be*
Here?

ANTHEMIA

On my morning shuffle commitment
Now, to my muscles, ankles, and knees.

From my hospital gown, my backside's pleas
For privacy gape, grimace, up the corridor floor.
I clutch the gown at the back with a twist
So that my wrinkled butt does not peep
With a roguish wink and snort and compete.
At what age, along the curve of life,
And when, will I no longer feel
Obligated to see beyond the routine
                              Deal
The mailbox I stroll up the front
Gravel drive to
Hands out   To me?
By whose decree
Will our America take six hundred years
                              More
To gestate in the womb of the Universe
To become fully born among history's
                              Lore?
We crossed into new territory
Overnight   In July, 2016
When Dallas' robot bomb slammed
                              Into smithereens
The lost phantom
                              That was Micah.
Just wait now until every soldier,
Vigilante, and street thug—Judah,
Ismail, Malidoma, Jill, and Jack—
Has one, or learns how to hack
Them out   Homemade,
Sliced from a home digital copier,
To rush to their neighbor's
                              Aid.
The Dallas bomb-out shows another problem
With the free open-carry pass practiced there,
                                    Soon, here.

Innocent opencarriers—twenty such practitioners—
Were arrested   On suspicion
During the Dallas shoot-out. One young man,
Brother of a protest organizer,
Turned himself in, to not become
                                 An instant suspect.
Once Micah's shooting had started,
                                 All the protesters
                                 Burned for cover
Around corners, behind cars,
Deep into   Doorways,
To save their lives as police officers
Turned toward the shooter to save lives
Of those who had run. Not a single citizen
                                 Carrying attempted
To hunt down the terrorist to take him out,
As the NRA claims will happen when we arm
                                 Citizens.
                                 This proves
Citizens carrying are equally open bullseyes
For police   And bangers
In open,   Outside space;
Targets to be arrested   Or slaughtered.
I wonder what would have
Happened in a Dallas theater or restaurant?
Would the twenty citizens
Carrying in a closed space
Have been able to take out
The rogue shooter in the balcony   Without hitting
                                      The stray innocent

Swirling and twirling   Around them
Like   Lost ammo?
                    How many officers
Must swallow bullets?
                    How many soldiers
Must absorb bullets and bombs?
                    How many
Young Black   Men's bodies
Must bend, fold, and fall?
How many funerals must women

Attend to even when it's not their own?
Eyeballs rolling across the tv or palmtop
Screen, I must stop keystroking to friends
Rounds and swirls of stuff I stumble upon
On   Presumptive
                            Nominees.
Let's hope we grab
A worthy servant as our next President. I am
Daily fixated on these lit echoes,
                            A fugue of indecision
                            And impulses,
Surrounded by open books I meant
To pay more attention to,
                            All the while clutching
A cracked book to my lap.
I am now watching   Congressional Hearings
With the FBI Director.
The Republicans   Hope to reveal
                         That shadowloving
Clinton cannot ever be trusted with secret
Or classified National files, folders,
                         And documents.
                         The sociopathetic Elephant
In the swamp   Is Haman.
He believes his lies, his only news source,
Ought to be true.
When we confess, we feel the unspoken force
Of knowing
He cannot be
                         Handed
Any nut or root   Or crumb
Of vital fruit.
I want to live forever but know I won't,
                         I can't.
Not without reimagined recognition
And sacrifice,
                         Nor the rant
                         From the vise
Of others.
The ground breaks at some point.

At some point the sky, the empty-armed
                         Shroud
Of crystal shards and twilight shrapnel,
                         Will fall in
                         Over me
During an Audi or Advil commercial.
                         Nowanights,
Falling into sleep, sensing an underwater
                         Knocking
At the door
Or   Tugging
At my   Underwear,
I, inert, strain and grunt awake in the dark.
If you wish to frighten me,
Threaten me with height
And water, for I cannot float.
Neither can I fly or swim
In the Unquenchable City
Of weaponized   Wear
                         And anger,
                         Still settling

City among street
Tributaries of mud   Where
We miscegenate
Pipe tobaccos, foods and
                         Spices
For the soul and table
                         And DNA
To aggravate outraged, aggrieved
Families.   Free at last.
Beneath our brain case,
With its ironclad
Escape hatch at all
Vectors, to catch the falling
Away of the quaint acacia
Clade's hallucinogens, and
Guttered prescriptions,
Consciousness is guaranteed.
                         At the occasional
Mid City   Cocktail hour

Pale voices break over stonewalls.
I abandon myself to a back
Receding room overhead that palls
The thinning air.
I've never liked the lair
Of standing around in a room
Like a lighthouse gazing
From familiar to stranger,
And even stranger faces
Vaporizing.
The world deigns to move

                  On faster

Still, across time,
An indulgence
Of noise and dust

               Spilling forth
               From our lips,
               Embalming

Our replacement

               Knees and hips.

In an abandoned
       Grassy gulch in New Orleans East
       In a Sunday morning park,
       A man's and woman's body can be
             Found.
Doesn't look like it just happened,
             Police say.

Should allegory
And symbol have
The vote?   Guns?
What have we   Run
To? For? From?
Body, mind, soul,
Spirit,   Each of which
Worries the world's Bound
Printer paper, printer
Ink, sacred language

             Itch.

I am no hawk nor balk,
No hulk nor sulk, nor
An easy silk walk
Out on a lark.
Of an East Ascension Graduation High School
                              Brawl, the
Police Chief says, They should all
Be blamed and ashamed!
I am happy that my life has lasted
Well into aches and pains.
I will not jinx my being by insisting
I will not die a young man's life.

AGAINST FORGETFULNESS

The Joseph-coated voices of our memory float
Among woods and forests, cross below, and skid

Along seas, oceans, lakes, and rivers to come to land
Renewed in the Asian Pacific, in all spaces specific

And subtle with reeds and syllables. If you do not
Understand, with a sigh

And gentleness close me shut, put me down, lay me
Aside, and forgive me for connecting with your

Great-grand descendants and not you.You will surely
Relive as and with them. History, never invertebrate,
Invisible and felt as the breeze, air, and fierce winds,
Over us move on, evolving, teaching human consciousness.

Whether we participate, as those written about here
Do, or experience our participation here as voyeurs
Of ourselves, as onlookers, or readers—we have
Obviously crossed a line in so many ways this year,
Having morphed toward a more outward expression
Of an awakening consciousness, fully knowing that Self—
Tselem, Nafsahu, Atma—Itself—is a welcoming myth.
Late in the night, on a Saturday, our local public channel
Plays back to back world myths: Lately, an hour of Jewish
New Orleans and of Greek New Orleans, heartened heart
Cultures, documentaries you may already be familiar with.
Myths underlie documentaries because history, a greater
Revisionist, moves to get out of the way so that we may
Witness with more clarity to welcome mythic communities
At our front and back yards within our own as our own.

I had never watched the first one before. Recently, after
Watching Jewish New Orleans for the first time, cold gin
Lifted from the freezer, colder over ice, I watched Greek
New Orleans—and went away knowing these two communities
Hold themselves in every local Black, Brown, Beige, Creole,

Cajun, Arab, Turkish, African grasp in common: a hypnotic averted
Fixation on local multicultural miscegenated bodies: similar local
    Histories of a people in diaspora
    Founding a home here:
Generations of Judean intermarriage and babies, a Kalamata insularity,
A place of worship, a national Judea, Greece, Yoruba, Gao, Ghana
Celebration cycle, a down but not out Post-Katrina community, on
    Strength to rebuild,
      And a love of New Orleans secret kitchen recipes.
        Trains, boats, sirens in the night air,
        Exactly what is it simmering below the surface
        Controlling what simmers above? Overturn bales
        Of straw toward me first, for my enemy is not an
        Ordinary people, not an innocent people in the haystack
        In the pyramid at the back, police sirens ululating,
        Ambulances wailing, ships' foghorns moaning
        On the River.
            An addiction to Self is a mist of numbers
            Floating over the pond of everything good
            And bad, decent and evil, a willful numbing,
            Not knowing anything at all.
        How many will die, overtaken by a cough?
        How insistent must a cough be from day to day
        To be an overtaking undertaker of the arts,
        Of a throat's life, breath, ego, soul, spirit,
        As the Self waiting expires waiting toward
            An aggregation of sunsets
        Expecting the male and female Holy One Blessed
            Be They at every
            Moment of origins?

BECCA LLAEID, LIFE IN HAND

My God, why write stories?!
                              Stories!
                              What a word!
If only we had a better word for the thing,
Life would be pleasanter! One might then feel
Useful in creating pieces. 'Story' seems so, so
Artificial a thing. Where I grew up, if someone accused
Me of telling a story, it meant I had lied before Heaven.
My father would be dishonored; my mother, shamed.
That's why I prefer sticking to the truth if I am going
To set some experience or observation down.
Otherwise, how could someone else trust it, truly?
But precisely how many sentences would it take
                              To speak the exact truth?
In fact, I am not sure why at this very moment I am
Compelled to record here what I intend to. It feels
Like a bowel movement, as if a thing has to pass
Out of me for me to feel cleansed, is what I think.
Or perhaps it's like giving birth, in order to feel
Whole again, and apart from the thing I yield.
Sometimes I think all I should do is just send
Random sentences out into the universe, to friends
And believers alike, as postcards,
                              In place of an intentional,
                              Wrought page or full manuscript.
Or perhaps the only writing I should accomplish is to scroll
With an ungloved finger a random sentence into the winter
Frost on a shop window as I am strolling through the chilled
Gray air along city streets.
                              I may seem to be exaggerating here a bit,
Because the only believer I know is Orriss, this lanky,
Redheaded white boy sprawled out on the sofa here, snoring,
Sound asleep. Actually, he's not really my husband, though
I think of him that way from time to time; not all the time, just
From time to time. But he's always my friend. He thinks of me
As his mulatto girlfriend. This is the way he recently identified
Me somewhere in the middle of the first paragraph he ever spoke
Online of me, but not in parentheses, of his very first web blog

That he constructed to help friends keep track of us while we are
Out and about here in the world away from home. What he doesn't
Know is that I am his Julatto Creole girlfriend. I in his, he's also
In my hands now, hands down!

THIS HOUSE DOES NOT BURN

We leave our body at every turn
Though the house does not burn
Dutifully up.

Faith is a belief in what does not even exist without evidence.
The evil we pursue against one another protects illusion.
Around me I sense myriad birds above, lowhigh and highlow,
And squirrels and rabbits scampering through the lush grasses
Of the pastures and paddocks, and the occasional black snake
Slithering away, out beneath the gates and fences.

Sometimes I can sleep only during the day, and so get nothing
Done, not much done anyway. At night, when I do sleep, I have
Beautiful, complex dreams I cannot remember when I wake.
I sense them, though, during the day, their content of pleasant people
Pioneering the air. It's like art whose frame reappears into the center
Of the canvas. Small towns and big families are the true Americana.
Homo Americanus ticks, but what makes each of us tick?
That is the question. I have lived in my head so much
All the decades of my life that I forget that life is a journey
And the journey all the while is home. Truth always lies
Within the extremes, along the periphery of chatter, clatter,
Chat, claptrap. What matters is what we are thinking now,
Then now, then again now. The self of our soul is always
Enlightened by two aspects along our autonomic nervous
System: a dark side and a bright side: the Dark and Bright
Enlightened Self of the Soul.

We can turn the switch on toward the dark
Or toward the bright. The choice is ours.
The choice is mine. The choice
Is our eager, pioneering personality's.

I always feel that I'm talking into a vacuum, or that others think
I'm a wild conspiracy suspicionist who should stop reading
And talking about tones across the world of spineless democracies
In retreat, as autocrats ignored and supported take center stage.
I don't believe everything I think. That's what I think.
Nor everything that others might think, for that matter.

My wife and I of some odd ninety years will one day through the portal
Leave. We have given one another, family and friends, the best years of
Our enclosures, before we cleave to death's embrace. Perhaps it won't be
Our choice at the time. It will just happen. My insurance cards are rapidly
Becoming unusable, ungratified by a government that has amortized
My life, assuming I, too, would have died by now. So I am no longer allowed
Special and expensive compounds. No sense in dipping into the coffers
Of the retirees younger than me, pharmacists say the government says.

> My wife used to accuse me of missing the forest
> For the trees. I have since realized that, yes,
> The trees are more interesting to me than the whole
> Forest. One should pay attention to individuals,
> Not an abstract or darkened wood.

This is the age of the Zika virus, of the rediscovery of the workings
Of LSD in the brain, of earthquakes, hurricanes, of more storms to come.
George Zimmerman is auctioning off the Kel-Tec PF-9 9mm firearm
He assassinated Trayvon Martin with when he rope-a-doped the lad
Into an altercation that landed Trayvon on top of him so he could shoot
Him chest to chest and not miss. Then he lied. Arm in arm. Chest to chest.
Then he lied

> Within our reach and grasp.

TELL THEM *ANAGNORISIS*

Tell them you don't want to write this poem.
Tell them you don't want to read this poem.

Tell them to write this poem.
Tell them to read this poem.

The barrier reefs softening away under
Thunderstorms out of the northwest,

How indecent, duplicitous with
Inner screaming indifference,
To imagine oneself imprisoned
In life when not in prison.

I do not recall when a definite
Something hardened in me,
Nitpicking its way into every
Personal and impersonal

Entice, Invite, Ignite, Incite.

If words are matter, what is their form?
What happens when I break off and take
Apart piece by piece their inner syllables
Of sound? Where outside of the state of
Experiences does our essential,
Fundamental form of being exist?

What is History when we shave it toward
A welter of words housing, protecting,
The uncertain, provisional, questing
Figuration of tyranny, paradox, absurdity,
Irony, ambiguity as a simultaneous, atonal
Surreal multivoiced counterpoint dragging
Tragedy toward our moment of recognition?

Will we in the end fall into one another
On a distant, deserted isle by the desire

Of love or by the lust of hatred, devouring
On spicy, or gagging on dry, boring, food
Of Life?

>Just what is the very nature of *being* if Jews, Kurds,
>Armenians, Asians, American Indians, Blacks, Berbers,
>Browns can be slaughtered *just for being*? Tell me.

MOTH MEMORY

New York's golden-chaired national child,
            Fool's gold at best,
Inaugurated two years ago, we have to pan
The stream, to sift out the interloping dross, the stench of words.
            I repeat myself.
I have often puzzled over why a pioneering moth or a garden gecko
Never recalls how to find its way out as it so inquisitively
            Confounded its way in, trapped between window
            And screen or along the wainscoting paneling of our
                Living room floor,
                Startled, wedged in, baffled,
                Back and forth
        Between perennial agnosticism and perennial wisdom,
            Folded in upon itself.

            Our next new civic duty, to keep an eye
            On the moral eunuchs in the House
And Senate, denies us the ease to become
Inured to the smirking, malignant shade and snicker
They barf and bark. They bear more watching than
The ManChild with The Joker's Grin, who implodes
            Every day, at times several times
            A day, with searing lies light
            Cannot ignore. His eunuchs implode
Upon the same agreed stick of dynamite up their
            Rectum each new morning
            To pose ahead of Freedom,
And Triumph Itself. Soon Everyone will run over
            One another, I am convinced. We
            Want to be alert enough to witness
The unbearable ruins among monuments.
            Haman has damaged his possible
            Statues in city squares with social
Justice activists worldwide, with Democracy's
            Intelligence; with China, with
        Germany, with Iran. At some
Point Greece, Israel, Saudi Arabia,
            And Turkey will push back against

    The exaggerated inexplicable that will
Damage them. They will have no choice.
    The stage is set. The cable screens
    Well lit glare. The Oval Office's four-year-old
Pouts everyday. Unlamented House Speaker crossed himself,
    Then gaveled the House into Session, masked
    Behind smiles across the indifferent Chamber
    Toward the Nation's dying. Though frustrated,
    Unlamented still, diffident bravery pricked him
    Only after early retirement.
When my mind changes me,
Reality never any longer
Becomes just an opinion.
    History repeats my words. I am no handwringing
    Harbinger. Join me here nonetheless. We
    Should watch, never to turn away when
    The only national speech so far this July
    To invade our skin invites hateful chants
    As it cries out in cornered, lost, self-hating
    Anguish from an un-presidential President's
    Mauling maw dripping as an open wound
    With lust for power, illiterate deceit, enabled
    By literate governmental cowards and late to
    School voters whom the President calls
    The uneducated whom he insists he loves.

PARTURITION

    Is   THIS
What dying Is, a bleeding Into life, what bedded
Down sounds like, a gargling, gurgling of rocks
Slipsliding along the throat, Keturah, shivering,
Wonders now, surrounded by friends and family
In the hotel breakfast lounge two days later, now
Afoot. I will be late for yoga, I know, she thinks,
And prayers if I don't bow away now. Ciao, she
Thinks to wave!

A kingdom for a robe's rope and a tree or else, her
Brain screams! How many millennia must we trust
Diving into another's dimming mirror to travel long
And far only to reach at the center angles of angels
Swarmed in shadows to find ourselves in our own
World, all the time there already? How many worlds
Kindled in the fires of desire, at long last annealed?

What Deity will doctor our spirit's wounds that we
May snatch our breath back from the sultry genome
Of generations of diversity's bloodletting entanglements
Among the noise and dust of indulgence, the falling
Away of the quaint measuring of rest and distance
Against forged golden gates tarnishing over time?
Her skin cracking with time shrivels and Keturah
Cackles into laughter and mirth.
          Cybercloaking minds, bodies, fingertips, fossil fuels,
          Monuments of ruins, all worlds move on, borders of
          Approximate absolutes abrading borders.

METAPHYSICS

Without an image opening, bridging, and closing
A gap, language drools in boring philosophy, empty
Metaphysics, useless epistemology. So I never pity
With the dying; only to the dead, who search for pith.
       Drop me off down on a planet of beauty
       And forgiveness. My body will rest awhile.
       My mind will roam its galaxy, its universe,
       Admire its suns and moons. I will squat awhile,
       A bit, without wheezing grunts and aches, to look
       To see all horizons, to hear and listen to all
       Murmurs and colors of every lasting, raging
       Moment of tender shower-driven winds
       Quantifying my qualifying eyes.
The Vagaries of human language, embedded
In the preterite, the present, and the future,
Grip the throat of students sifting for Self
In the preterist, the presentist, and the futurist
Emerging as a single immediacy of enclosures
       Startling through.

NO ATTITUDE

That's how consciousness works.

Blood takes sides in a neighborhood's
Attic, basement, stairwell, alleyway;
Under houses and porches where children
Hide, giggle and play.

      Who are you?
      What are you?

      Inner anger leads
      Neither to answers
      Nor to responses.

      Anger masks Sad.
      Noun masks Verb.

      All of Life, the Predicate
      Itself, though as chained
      Tense, and circumlocution,
      In all its forms, masks
      Time unchained in freefall.

      Falling
      Free,
Downloading freedom from the air we breathe,
From the sky we take in, without attitude.

AGONISTES, ROOTLESS, ADRIFT IN POINT COUPÉ

What is there about our interaction
After independence? Knowing us
First, when each of the other roamed
Independent, who can describe us now,
Our entanglement perfecting joy's
Imperfection?

I imagine togetherness now
Rewriting the separateness
Of times before. Invoking
Nothing at all about separation
Or future partings as back
And forth span casual voids
Of empty times, of space
Emptying out.

Still I feel undefeated
And defeated by search,
Not *a* search but by
The relentless verb itself,
Queen and goddess of words,
Cresting above the blood brain
Baring straits of my mind embracing
The joys of uncertainty as well.

As well, seas are rising, swelling
Asunder cities and coves; wildfires'
Sparks cloaked in sawdust, earthen
Dust drowning over stonewalling
Human existence, boiling anger's
Water-laden blood on low ground
Into next century.

Enemy complexity turns us
Away staring back without
Blinking while simplicity
Beckons us in in familiar

Voice. Listening in, we
Never choose. See in, I
Plead. Listen then. Only
Then, on the inside, by
Choice free, but never
Choosing.

I am no therapeutic fugue.
I won't ensnare anyone
With more than a series
Of queries revealing a
Contradictory Self. Nothing
Should hide away in a safe
Sunk beneath a dead sea's
Reign.

My Reine proud to no longer
Be attending morning prayer
On demand and command
In the same sweaty pews
Invisible alphabetically ranged,

How can she disappear to let
The voices come forth first
as if she notices nothing's edges?
Hearing everything, she looks,
She notices, she sees. She is my
Secret seeing ear perking up at
Every age.

Who are we stardust scattered?

Who am I?
I am Who I Am
That Black Uptown
Third Ward New
Orleans Housed
Only Son.

What am I?
I Am What I Am
Those fifty Thousand
Years of West African,
Six generations of Eastern
European, blood
And thunder aneled.

Long for a quantum beginning, Bang or Bounce,   ·
Once again from Nothing to
Something, for next time.

Seas of anxiety against influence,
Inharmonious digital distractions,
Violence international,
Social and political,
Crest.

EULALIA AT THE FIRST WAILING WALL

Preborn, borderless, the first to daven
At the backbone of their mother's womb,
Babies breach time and space, particles
And waves, fields and streams, galaxies
And universes, crossing frontiers to pass
Through gates, to become exactly us,
Though evolved, not as leftover fossils
As we are when they come. They arrive
More new, transformed, yet not knowing
They need us, until they blink before their
First light behind eye opening curiosity.

"Lalia!" we beckon, as others and we
Wreathe around her, smile at her, a crescent
Moon in the crook of her mother's arm. She
Yawns. We lean in. Without evidence on her
Third day here, we tell each other she's now
Smiling at us also. I imagine her leaning in
Also, before birth, breathing nutrients for life
From our daughter's womb. She did not turn
Down headfirst. She came to us breech,
A survivor of nine months, holding on just
Enough, tall already, to sense an unfamiliar
Safe awe against the ballast of the left uterine
Wall, the right one deflated, in her first liftoff
And drift through space, and enters history
Where the past waits and gives way: humanity
Restored and visible, soon to be starving for
Revelations in colostrum and milk.